FROM CHRIST'S VIEW, I AM FREE NOW

FROM CHRIST'S VIEW, I AM FREE NOW

10 Ways to Understand Our True Freedom

Florence A. Roberts

Disclaimer: This book contains my insights from my continuing study of the Bible and Science and Health with Key to the Scriptures by Mary Baker Eddy. These insights have given me a new way of thinking about the different areas of life. The new view is helping me realise a more satisfying and peaceful life. The truths that are working for me have been around for many years, but their practicality and benefits are grossly underestimated, perhaps not appreciated enough, and therefore unused. Though I do not make any representations here that what I am sharing is a guarantee for everyone who reads this book, I do know that when people in sincerity and honesty endeavour to understand and love God, as Science and Health explains these concepts, they realise healing in their lives. I have done my best to share what I am learning. I hope that others can achieve a greater sense of peace if they awaken to the truth about who we are and our relationship with God. I do not make any warranties with respect to the completeness, and life changes everyone can experience from reading this book. I disclaim any warranties implied or expressed. I shall in no event be held liable for any loss or any damages, including but not limited to special, incidental, consequential, or other damages. I do know that for some, this awakening, from the sincere and honest study of the Bible and Mrs. Eddy's book, will make a difference. I trust that some shared insights will lead others to the answers they are seeking and encourage them to engage in their own study to gain understanding for their spiritual growth. I can say that the more understanding I gain about the nature of God, the more I realise my own freedom now.

ISBN (paperback): 979-8-9932359-0-5

ISBN (ebook): 979-8-9932359-1-2

Book design and production by www.AuthorSuccess.com

DEDICATION

This book is dedicated to all Truth seekers, my parents,
John Justice, Hannah Adoley Fletcher, and my dear sister Justina.

CONTENTS

INTRODUCTION

*And Ye shall Know The Truth,
and The Truth Shall Make You Free.*

John 8:32

Christ Jesus

The Bible and the Christian Science textbook, *Science and Health
with Key to the Scriptures* by Mary Baker Eddy, contain a road map
for all to understand our true freedom, what we are meant to have.

"What is the permanent solution?" asked a relative who
had been struggling for years with persistent stomach
problems. I had tried before to share some of the spiritual insights that
had helped me, but he never seemed open to listening. Finally, tired
of suffering, he asked the question in earnest.

Confidently, I responded, "The answer is our willingness to yield
to God with our whole hearts, and to the truth about who He, the only
Creator, says we are." My own life had changed profoundly when I
started to understand who God is, and who I am in relation to Him.

This book you are reading outlines a practical understanding
and application of God's incredible Truth, Love, and Healing Power
as revealed in the Holy Bible. In 1866, after an accident that seemed
certain to end her life, a devout Christian woman gained a life-saving

insight into how the message and ministry of Christ brought about healing. That insight not only saved her in that moment, but it also liberated her from a lifetime of affliction.

After years of prayerful study and deep exploration, she published the first edition of her findings in a book titled *Science and Health with Key to the Scriptures.* This book, written by Mary Baker Eddy, has become a beloved classic and a trusted companion to Bible study. The spiritual truths she uncovered, while seeking to overcome her own challenges, have helped people around the world find freedom from various difficulties and overcome seemingly insurmountable obstacles.

Sometime earlier in my own life, I picked up *Science and Health with Key to Scriptures* after a Christian Science practitioner read passages from it to my father, who at the time was believed to be dying. By God's grace, my father recovered and lived seventeen more years, until his passing in 1992.

The memory of my father's and sister's healing from asthma encouraged me to seek a deeper understanding of my relationship with God. At the time, I was married with three children and working as a registered medical nurse. Outwardly, I appeared to be managing a full life—but inwardly, everything felt off. I was constantly anxious about the future and deeply dissatisfied. My husband and I were unhappy. We faced financial difficulties, and I lived under a constant sense of pressure, trying to juggle my career, household responsibilities, child-rearing, and daily obligations.

In earlier years, I had searched for answers in positive thinking and self-help books. The Bible, however, had always been my anchor. As a child, I had attended Sunday school, where I was taught to memorize the Psalms so I could pray when needed. Most Bible stories were familiar to me, and they continued to offer comfort and calm whenever I read them.

Yet self-doubt often overshadowed my decisions. I carried a persistent sense of lack—lack of money, courage, and confidence. This lack held me back from seizing good opportunities, and I often suffered from self-condemnation. I postponed my joy, believing that something had to happen before I could be happy. I tried to please others, even when it compromised my own peace and happiness. I lacked the courage to stand firmly in Truth and trust in its power over all things.

What I needed was something that would free me from the grip of constant anxiety and sadness, something that would bring a lasting sense of peace. I found this when I chose to return to the study of *Science and Health with Key to the Scriptures,* along with Mrs. Eddy's other writings and articles by other Christian thinkers inspired by her work. In those pages, I discovered something I had entirely missed during the many years I called myself a Christian.

What needless fear! The anxiety I suffered was, at times, so severe that it left me exhausted. I had been taught to pray, but my prayers brought only limited comfort—they were prayers without understanding. I reached outward for God, imagining Him as "that man sitting up there." I do not think I truly believed my prayers.

When I began reading *Science and Health with Key to the Scriptures,* something remarkable happened: I no longer woke up from a nap with horrible anxiety and a sense of impending doom. This marked a profound shift from the deep anxiety I had carried for years. Slowly, a desire stirred in me—a longing to share what was being revealed. For the first time, I was gaining a deeper understanding of those scriptural messages I had grown up hearing.

I began to wonder: Why had no one clearly explained the unchanging fact that we are children of God? Why was I never taught Christ Jesus's Truth with the same clarity and confidence used to teach the principles of arithmetic? If I misunderstand math, my calculations will be wrong. Similarly, when our foundational understanding of humanity is flawed, the result is confusion, suffering, and misdirection. Many of life's woes stem not from external forces, but from the tangle of our own wrong thinking. A correct understanding of God's nature might have spared me countless tears, mistakes, and sleepless nights.

If I am God's reflection, that Truth was never made clear. If God is Love itself, I have never heard it in a way that reached my heart. If God is Truth, that understanding completely escaped me. And so, I lived feeling separate from Him. For that, I paid the price. To have begun with a proper foundation might have spared me many ills— some so painful, it has taken years to "unknow" them.

When a friend told me about her brother's diagnosis of cancer, I wanted so much to share with her that many people had found healing simply by reading Mrs. Eddy's book. But I knew she would have nothing to do with it. She would never pass it on to her brother. So, I listened, quietly, with deep regret—because I knew I could not help him with what I knew.

I could not really blame her. What I was learning required a radical willingness to reconsider everything we have been taught to believe about who we are. My friend had visited me twice before and noticed the book I was reading. The first time, she made a face. The second time, she picked it up, glanced at the title, and set it back down without a word.

Around the same time, another friend stopped by my store. She had just been diagnosed with breast cancer and was frightened. As she shared the news, I did not feel alarmed. Something deeper stirred in me—a quiet certainty—and a Bible verse I had been praying with: "What do ye imagine against the Lord? He will make an utter end: affliction shall not rise up the second time" (Nahum 1:9). I spoke with conviction, sharing what I was beginning to understand: that God's pure Love for His children could not allow any illness to afflict His own. Then I gave her a copy of Mrs. Eddy's book.

A few weeks later, she returned—more relaxed, her usual smile back—and thanked me. She told me she had been praying with that verse and continuing to see her doctor, and that everything was all right. She returned the book, though I cannot recall why, and I did not press her. By then, I had learned that many people form opinions about Mrs. Eddy's writings without giving them the prayerful study they require.

Not long after that, I left the state to study a healing ministry rooted in a deeper spiritual understanding of the Bible. In the process, I lost touch with my friend, though I thought of her often.

One day, while visiting home, I stopped by the local market. I had just picked up a carton of eggs and was heading towards the fish counter when I ran into her husband. His expression changed as soon as he recognized me. He told me she had passed away a few months earlier. Then he added, quietly, that she had asked to see me, but he had not known how to reach me.

You can imagine my grief and disappointment. I had no words that could adequately express what I felt. After we parted, I carried a heavy guilt—partly because I could not make her see the importance of continuing, of claiming her birthright as a child of God. And yet

I also knew what I was learning could not be forced on anyone. The Truth is, Mrs. Eddy's book requires a humble, sincere heart, one that truly longs to understand God.

Over time, I came to see that even when people reject the insights into divine Love and Truth revealed in Christian Science, they often agree with the underlying principles when I speak to them using the language of traditional faith. What I offered was not so much a departure from belief, but a return—a new approach to life that applies, in practical ways, the very scriptural messages Jesus came to teach.

Life is spiritual. Each person is on their own journey, and only one Truth makes us free. Some have already discovered it and are on their way toward fuller realization. Others have been awakened through their Love for God and for others. Still others are actively seeking.

When Jesus was asked when the kingdom of God would come, he said, "The kingdom of God cometh not with observation: Neither shall they say, Lo here! or lo there! for, behold, the kingdom of God is within you:" (Luke 17:20-21). If the Kingdom of God is within us, then it follows that as we discover who we truly are, we will find it. This is the kingdom we are instructed to seek first, so that all other things may be added unto us.

Later in Luke, we read, "Whosoever shall not receive the kingdom of God as a little child shall in no wise enter therein" (Luke 18:17). The kingdom of God is revealed to those who carry the innocence of a child—those who are ready to accept what is shown to them. Only those willing to let go of false conceptions, and who possess that childlike readiness to yield to the truth, can fully receive what Jesus came to teach.

Just think—one right teaching, planted in the fertile, innocent, and receptive heart of a child, could prevent a lifetime of mistakes.

Despite all the degrees I have earned after my name, the most satisfying title I hold is one I paid no money to receive: "Unlimited Child of God." I once heard an inspired Christian healer use that phrase, and it left a lasting impression on me. I like to remind myself of it often, because I know it belongs not only to me but to everyone. We either do not yet know it, or we prefer to be defined by the other titles we collect along the way. But the word *unlimited* speaks to a freedom that means more to me than any credential.

There is so much struggle among nations and individuals. Could it be that we are all trying to be something we were never meant to be? People seem to find greater peace when they choose a spiritual path, regardless of their background or beliefs. We come from different cultures, speak different languages, carry different views, and wear different faces, yet we all stem from one infinite Source.

We must learn to deny false beliefs and instead, with humility and confidence, affirm what Paul declared: that nothing can separate us from the Love of God, and that in Him we live and move and have our being. (Romans 8:38-39, Acts 17:28). We are always in His presence. Just as our shadows never leave us, so we remain forever within the presence of God. And to me, that is deeply comforting.

Christ Jesus came to teach us our spiritual perfection—and the power that perfection includes. We cannot be reflections of the perfect original if we continually accept the flawed, material images we have been taught to believe. Every mistaken belief we accept becomes another layer of dust, obscuring our view of the divine clarity and perfection we are meant to reflect. Scripture reminds us again and again that we are one with God. Why, then, do we not obey this truth?

Why do we so often place our trust in what medical science tells us, rather than in the Word that declares our oneness with the Creator?

Can we honestly say we Love God while denying His magnificence, His power, and His allness? Can we call ourselves children of God and still cling to the belief that we are inherently flawed or broken? This misrepresentation of who we are keeps us imprisoned, locked in a false narrative. Too often, we deceive ourselves just enough to feel comfortable in the dream. But how many of us are truly happy living by beliefs that bring fear, pain, or sorrow?

We are "Unlimited Children of God, Ever in His Presence." This Truth brings peace and answers many of our most profound questions. Understanding dissolves the fears, doubts, and anxieties we often carry.

We inherit this birthright when we learn to recognize God's ever-presence, His protecting power, and His infinite Love. This understanding teaches us to go to God first for every answer. It is God who heals all our seeming diseases. He is immediately available, no matter where we are or what confronts us. We begin to know ourselves truthfully by unlearning the many falsities we have accepted about who we are. We have a powerful promise: we are never separated from the Love of God. We only need to remember this Truth at all times, and to rejoice and give thanks for such grace.

But knowing this Truth is not possible when my thoughts are full of false concepts about life. The human mind cannot perceive the spiritual man of God's creation. This is why Scripture urges us to have the same mind that was in Christ Jesus (Phil. 2:5). Jesus had the Christ Mind, which enabled him to see man's perfection at all times.

So, we, too, must re-educate our thinking. We must spiritualize our thoughts. This transformation comes by seeking the Truth, studying it consistently, understanding it deeply, loving it enough to live it, and trusting it fully. This is what is helping me cultivate spiritual discernment—to recognize the "I," the real man, who is spiritual and now free.

I have written *this* book to help awaken Truth seekers to what they already possess. My hope is to inspire people to study the Bible more deeply and to discover its spiritual significance through the sincere, honest, and persistent study of *Science and Health with Key to the Scriptures* by Mary Baker Eddy, used as a companion to Scripture.

Through these passages, readers will gain:

- A greater understanding of how to overcome fear
- A deeper awakening to the Truth that you are a reflection of God, continually in His presence—and how this transforms every area of your life
- A richer understanding of the nature of God
- A powerful, spiritually grounded approach to prayer
- Practical ways to apply Jesus' message to daily living
- Insights into how you can experience better health, greater peace, and lasting contentment
- A clearer view of the true meaning of humility

Let us see what insights we will gain from our next chapter on **WHO AM I?**

CHAPTER ONE

WHO AM I?

"Beloved, Now Are We The Sons Of God . . . "
1 John 3:2

"Cease ye from man, whose breath is in his nostrils:
for wherein is he to be accounted of?"
Isaiah 2:22

"Know ye that the Lord he is God: it is he that hath made us, and
not we ourselves; we are his people, and the sheep of his pasture."
Psalms 100:3

I have often asked myself, "Who am I?" Knowing what the Bible says, I always answered truthfully that I am a beloved child of God--but I did not fully understand what God says about who is truly His child. Since we are all of one Father, as Malachi says, "Have we not all one father? hath not one God created us?" (Mal. 2:10), then I should see everyone, everywhere, as a child of God.

As I studied the Bible and its spiritual interpretation from the Christian Science textbook *Science and Health with Key to the Scriptures* by Mary Baker Eddy, I saw clearly that I had entertained a limited view of God all these years. In order to embrace the Truth about God, I had to give up the false notion of Him as a man somewhere and accept the infinite, spiritual nature of God. Although this was not easy to do, it made perfect sense.

I am amazed at how contradictory the two accounts of creation are, once pointed out. And yet, no one ever explained that. I grew up believing the mortal sense of creation without question, even though the Bible clearly begins with the spiritual version:

Gen. 1:26, 27, and 31 partially quoted here, states, "And God said, let us make man in our own image, after our likeness: . . . .So God created man in his own image, in the image of God created he him; male and female created he them . . . And God saw everything that he had made, and behold, it was very good."

The second chapter gives the account of the mist going up, the creation of man from dust, and the formation of woman from man's rib. Then, after saying that all He created was "very good," God is now depicted as cursing man, foretelling suffering.

I am not a Bible scholar, but through my study, I've come to understand that the opposing views of creation in the first and second chapters of Genesis cannot both be correct. If God is Spirit, then creation made in His likeness must be spiritual. If God is wholly good, then His creation must also be good. He wouldn't create a sinful mortal, watch him suffer, or make His own likeness capable of doing things that are incompatible with His likeness.

It was also becoming clear to me that a finite God could not be everywhere at all times—and yet this had been my unquestioned view of God for most of my life.

The more I prayed—humbly and sincerely—to understand the nature of God, the more was revealed. God's intangible, infinite qualities become tangible *in action*. If God is All and is only good, then all good qualities must express Him. All people, then, are the expression, image, witness, reflection, and idea of God. In reality, we all possess the qualities that make up the nature of God.

This understanding of God is critical. A Christian healer once explained the idea this way: "To refer to ourselves as the small *i*, which always has something hanging over the top of it, is to identify ourselves wrongly." It's a funny analogy, but it helped me see something. Maybe that's why people say, 'There is always something." They come to expect there will always be something wrong with business, relationships, school, health, or the world.

I used to wonder, *What else could go wrong*? That kind of worry assumes that wrong is normal. Some people think constant worry is just being cautious. I know many who always expect that things will go wrong—and for them, it often does.

Pessimistic thinking is sinful because it denies the allness of God and ignores the command, " . . . .be not afraid." (John 6:20). It gives power to fear and discord, disobeying the First Commandment: "Thou shalt have no other gods before me." (Ex 20:3). That command means I should not let anything preoccupy my thought more than God.

The acceptance of many false beliefs about life kept me from realizing true mental freedom. But my growing readiness to accept that God is All—that His creation reflects Him and is entirely good—has helped me to understand, without question, who I truly am. The Bible says, "And God saw everything that He had created and behold it was very good" (Gen 1:31).

Further enlightenment through *Science and Health with Key to the Scriptures* broadened my understanding of the nature of God. God is Mind, Spirit, Soul, Principle, Life, Truth, and Love. This understanding helped me accept the spiritual nature of God and begin to see myself as the reflection of such infinite qualities.

The Bible refers to God as Mind: intelligent, wise, and all-knowing . . . . we have the mind of Christ" (1 Cor. 2:16). This Mind is the infinite intelligence that knows nothing imperfect about His own child.

God as Spirit: real substance, grace, and goodness. "God is a Spirit: and they that worship Him must worship him in spirit and in truth" (John 4:24).

God as Soul: beauty, grandeur, harmony, and tranquillity. "Behold, all souls are mine; as the soul of the father, so also the soul of the son is mine" (Ezek. 18:4).

God as Principle: just, orderly, punctual, balanced, and courageous. "He is the Rock, his work is perfect: for all his ways are judgment" (Deut. 32:4). And later, " . . . he is excellent in power, and in judgment, and in plenty of justice:" (Job 37:23).

God as Life: lively, energetic, full of vitality, and joyful. "The Lord is the strength of my life; of whom shall I be afraid?" (Ps. 27:1) Another Psalm declares, "That thy way may be known upon earth, thy saving health among all nations" (Ps. 67: 2).

God as Truth: honest, trustworthy, truthful, pure, and faithful. Deut. 32:4 calls Him "... a God of truth and without iniquity, just and right is he."

God as Love: compassionate, loving, and affectionate. 1John. 4:8 says, "He that loveth not knoweth not God; for God is love."

It is this fresh view of the nature of God that has awakened me to my genuine selfhood. 2 Corinthians 4:18 says, "... we look not at the things which are seen, but at the things which are not seen: for the things which are seen are temporal; but the things which are not seen are eternal."

As I strove to make these divine attributes real in my own life, I felt led to read a lecture by Herbert E. Rieke, C.S.B., titled "Discovering Peaceful Relationships." In it, Mr. Rieke shared a story from his time as an army chaplain, during an informal religious service held on a convalescent ward. To help illustrate the concept of the perfect man, the group chose the subject of "Women" for the discussion. Naturally, this topic caught the attention of all the men present.

Mr. Rieke began by asking them what they desired in the women they hoped to marry. At first, the men focused on physical beauty—until one of them spoke up and said, "Beauty is not everything." Then another added, "I don't want a wife who is dumb." So Mr. Rieke turned the discussion toward the value of intelligence. They all agreed they wanted a wife with wisdom and understanding.

Next, he asked, "What if the woman was intelligent and beautiful, but hateful and mean?" The men quickly agreed that they would not want a woman like that. They wanted someone who expressed love, compassion, tolerance, and the ability to forgive.

So, he asked, "What if she had all of those qualities, but did not express truth?" They all agreed again—no one wanted a wife who could not be trusted because she lied. Everyone wanted someone who would be true to them.

Finally, he posed one more question: "What if she had no life in her; if she was lazy and boring, had no enthusiasm, and was indifferent?"

Of course, they all wanted someone who would be energetic, lively, engaging, and active. Then one man said he did not want someone with *too much* life, who would run to clubs all night long. He hoped for someone who loved her home, good books, flowers in the garden, and children.

They all recognized that these were deeper, spiritual interests—qualities that expressed *Soul*. They agreed on the importance of depth, spiritual poise, and harmony: the unseen beauty that is felt rather than seen on the outside. Each man also agreed that his wife-to-be would need to express fairness, orderliness, balance, and good grooming—for these are qualities of principle.

With the healer's help, they came to see that it is the Spirit that satisfies—and that those are the spiritual qualities God has given to each of His children. They are eternal realities, and all can allow their expression.

At the end of this discussion, the men asked where they could find such a girl. To that, the healer asked, "What kind of a man would such a girl be looking for?" They all burst out laughing. Of course, the answer was clear: she would be looking for a husband who possessed those very same qualities. With this, they saw that with these qualities, they identify the complete child of God.

God's child, as His reflection, never lacks anything—because good health, wisdom, love, proper judgment, moral courage, wealth, intelligence, energy, humility, patience, and joy are included in the eternal qualities of God's nature, and therefore in man's true nature.

Paul said, "Nothing can separate us from the love of God" (Rom. 8:39). That statement means nothing if we think of ourselves as what God is not. If we see ourselves as limited mortals, we can never be receptive to spiritual truth.

We are always in the presence of God. Just as we can never be separated from our own shadows, every drop of the ocean is always part of the whole ocean. I find this spiritual fact very comforting.

"I am a felon," was the ready answer a young man gave me when I asked him to register to vote. He was telling the Truth about what he had come to believe, but what struck me as both surprising and sad was the ease with which he said it. This has become his identity.

Because he thought of himself as a felon, I feared he might do something else consistent with that belief before his probationary period ended. He might always remain a felon. He could have simply said, "I cannot vote," and then explained why. But instead, he led with the label.

Does the system truly understand why the rate of recidivism is so high?

Accepting any limitation is disobedience to God. If I dwell on the fact that I am a woman and accept any limitations that come with that, I am disobeying God—because that is not how He knows me. If I affirm that I am shy, unworthy, timid, resentful, or revengeful, then I suffer from being all the things that God has *not* created as part of me.

The power of Truth displaces all the lies about who I am, so I can fully see the loving, worthy, deserving, obedient, and beloved child of God that He knows.

I am "an Unlimited Child of God, Ever in His Presence." This knowledge has helped to erase many of the fears, doubts, and anxieties I used to carry. I own my birthright as a child of God. Learning to be grateful for God's everlasting presence, His protecting power, and His infinite Love helps me turn to God first—for all my answers.

Why was it so challenging for me to accept this truth? To be honest, I felt unworthy to be identified with God. Jesus taught that

Truth makes us free—the Truth of our true, perfect spiritual being. He made clear that this perfect identity was for everyone to claim. "Be ye therefore perfect, as your Father which is in heaven is perfect." (Matt. 5:48). Each step I take toward fully realizing this Truth brings me more peace and freedom.

The more convinced I become of the power of the Truth, the more readily the Truth comes to my consciousness when I am faced with a problem. I no longer merely talk about the truth—I feel it and apply it.

I am so grateful for this step forward, because I used to believe my problems were bigger than the power of God. But I must continue in this new way of thinking, whether I am confronted with challenges or things seem to be going just fine.

In the Bible, a man named Nicodemus asked Jesus how He performed His miracles. Jesus told him he would have to be born again. Nicodemus, taking this literally, did not understand. Jesus explained what He meant by being born again. He said, " . . . Except a man be born of water and of Spirit he cannot enter into the kingdom of God" (John 3:5).

This birth of the Spirit is the acceptance of your spiritual identity as a child of God.

I realised I had been living a Life full of contradictions. When I respected and Loved someone, I listened to the good things they told me and tried to follow their advice. But I had been doing the opposite with God. I professed to Love Him, but I was not obeying His laws.

I had to surrender my personal will and recognize that God already had a perfect plan for my Life. I must not accept any discord as real. Discord is healed by the establishment of Truth in my consciousness—and that Truth reveals just how unreal the discord truly is.

I used to pray by asking God to grant my self-willed requests. But over time, I've learned a different way. Now, instead of pleading, I spend quiet time alone with God, simply *knowing* His presence with all my heart. In that stillness, I seek to feel His power and presence. That sacred quietude fills me with inspiration, often leading to practical answers to my questions. In this way of praying, I humbly and fully acknowledge that all good comes from God.

I often examine my thoughts and actions to understand better where I may be indifferent, disobedient, disrespectful, or ungrateful toward God. We read, "If ye love me, keep my commandments" (John 14:15). It is not enough to profess my Love for God—I must *prove* it.

For example, I ask myself whether I am judging others based on skin colour or nationality. I do this because I recognize how deeply the world clings to false beliefs about these things. If I am to be obedient to God, I must make a conscious effort to see His creation in every human. We are all brothers and sisters; in Truth, there are no enemies.

I desire understanding—no matter the cost. This hunger leads me to a deeper grasp of what it means to "rejoice in tribulation." God is always present, and confusion is only temporary. Every conflict offers an opportunity for spiritual growth. With that conviction, I welcome challenges, knowing God is helping me through them.

As the Bible tells us in Matthew 5:8, "Blessed are the pure in heart, for they shall see God." For me, purity means striving to keep my thoughts clear. I cannot hold on to sadness, self-condemnation, or self-doubt and, at the same time, perceive the beauty, grandeur, and harmony of God's presence. One must give to the other.

Jesus said, "But seek ye first the kingdom of God... and all these things shall be added unto you" (Matthew 6:33). To discern how faithfully I am following this command, I ask myself a few search-ing questions: Am I beginning my day with God? Am I turning completely to Him for answers? Am I striving to express only those qualities that reflect His nature?

Psalm 17:15 declares, "As for me, I will behold thy face in righ-teousness: I shall be satisfied, when I awake, with thy likeness." What a promise—that when I truly awaken to the Truth of my identity as God's likeness, I will be satisfied and free. Similarly, Deuteronomy 6:5 reminds me, "... And thou shalt love the Lord thy God with all thine heart, and with all thy soul, and with all thy might." These verses remind us just how wholly God calls for our attention and devotion.

Isaiah 31:1 warns against leaning on material solutions: "Woe to them that go down to Egypt for help ... "—a vivid image of misplaced trust. Instead, Romans 8:9 reassures us, "But ye are not in the flesh, but in the Spirit, if so be that the Spirit of God dwell in you." These words help me remember that my true Life is found in the Spirit, not in matter.

Still, have you ever noticed how easy it is to have more faith in a problem than in the power of God's Love to heal it? I experienced this when I was struggling with physical pain. I prayed, affirming my identity as God's child, knowing that such pain could not possibly be a part of me. As I spent time thinking about my perfection, I sud-denly realised I still had more faith in the reality of the pain than in God and the reality of my perfection.

I burst out laughing when it finally dawned on me: I had been trying to be *humanly* spiritual. I was not thinking of myself as the reflection of God, and therefore, perfect. I was still seeing myself as a mortal, while claiming spiritual Truth as my own. It was an awakening to realise that spiritual perfection must be my starting point in order to correctly counter any discord. I prayed by lifting my thoughts with the truth about my spiritual being. As I stayed with these truths, I felt the pain easing—until eventually, I could no longer feel the disturbing sensation.

It is also helpful to understand the concept of the infinity of God. Since God is infinite, all His qualities are equally present. This means I can be courageous, loving, strong, and beautiful. I can have abundance, affection, and honesty. And I know everyone else can express all these qualities at the same time, too. I can be sure of having an everlasting supply of whatever I need. Can infinity ever end? The answer, obviously, is no.

Since God is infinite, the discord we face is not real. This teaches me to seek God first for every answer—always holding on to perfection and recognizing the lie of material circumstances. Hence, in healing, we are *always* healing wrong beliefs. The Truth we claim replaces and vanquishes false belief, not the material circumstance. It is essential to keep the spiritual value of all things in mind.

So, for example, if my marriage is discordant, I am still somehow holding on to the belief that my husband can be selfish, immoral, or dishonest. But God tells us to leave the material dream for the truth. If I continue to seek my answers from my own and others' opinions, I am either still ignorant of the spiritual reality or I am choosing to disobey its cautions.

If our experience reflects our thoughts, does it not make sense to heal the thoughts that are out of alignment with the Truth? It is a mistaken belief that man can be forgetful, or that a home can be vulnerable or exposed. It is not people we must correct, but the belief that anyone can be dishonest, unjust, or deceitful. We must take care not to be distracted by appearances before our eyes.

This is why it is essential to anchor ourselves in the presence of perfection. The Bible exhorts us, "Be ye therefore perfect, even as your Father which is in heaven is perfect" (Matthew 5:48). This is not a future hope—it is a present Truth. I am not waiting for a shift in circumstances to reveal my perfection, nor is it something I grow into over time. Our spiritual wholeness is already established. Perfection is a present fact, here and now.

I was sitting in the congregation at a burial service in Ghana when I heard the preacher speak of a future, eternal happiness. This idea of rest in the hereafter had been part of my early Christian education. But eternity is ceaseless; all that is truly good is eternal—present here and now.

Subtle misrepresentations and their implied contradictions can lead us into wicked beliefs that supplant spiritual realities. These beliefs cannot be ignored. Even seemingly simple assumptions can slip in unnoticed—such as the notion that if I am hurt, I must wait for relief. Yet we are taught that God is an ever-present help, more immediate than any material remedy.

If Jesus was the Son of God, then we, too, as God's image, must see ourselves as such and follow His example. His understanding of God's allness—His power, presence, wisdom, and Love—was his source. It was his supply, His medicine for healing every discord, his everything.

The following verses emphasize the value of spirituality and the blessing of relinquishing every false belief to attain it: " . . . the kingdom of heaven is like unto a merchant man, seeking goodly pearls: Who, when he had found one pearl of great price, went and sold all that he had and bought it" (Matthew 13:45, 46). And in Romans 8:6-7: "For to be carnally minded is death; but to be spiritually minded is life and peace. Because the carnal mind is enmity against God." False suggestions—those originating in the human mind that attempt to displace the omnipotence of God—are indeed enmity to Him.

Understanding who I am took time. Trusting that understanding and living it means the work of a lifetime—and I am glad to do it. There is no terrible struggle in this when we are willing to accept this uplifting concept of self. Paul urged us, " . . . be ye transformed by the renewing of your mind that ye may prove what is that good, and acceptable, and perfect will of God" (Romans 12:2).

When I ceased my inner warfare and humbly placed my feet in His footprints, I began to feel the peace that has always been mine. Peace in any relationship starts with the peace we cultivate within. When I dwell on negativity—about myself or someone else—I affirm its reality. If I accept that another is poor or sick, I make space for that false belief in my thought, as well. Eventually, it may try to take form in my own experience.

This is why obedience to the commandment to Love our neighbour is essential to our harmony. Holding false beliefs about others also binds us to those same illusions. Wherever we encounter wrong, we are called to deny its reality—because it does not belong to the Kingdom of God within us.

"Whosoever is born of God doth not commit sin; for his seed remaineth in him: and he cannot sin, because he is born of God" (1 John 3:9). We are constantly misled by the five physical senses. That is why must remain aware of our spiritual identity in order to see the truth. If I do not stay awake to the truth, I fall for the 1+1=3 premise. The solution is wrong. Our highest calling, then, is to remain awake to our true selfhood.

Each day, I must consciously see in myself—and in everyone else—the wisdom and intelligence of Mind, the substance and reality of Spirit, the beauty and harmony of Soul, the strength and justice of Principle, the vitality and freshness of Life, the purity and innocence of Truth, and the absolute perfection and loveliness of Love. When I meet every circumstance—whether sickness, unhappiness, or lack—with such a viewpoint, I begin to live what Jesus promised: whoever believes in Him will do the works He did also.

Let us see what insights we will gain from our next chapter on **LOVE.**

CHAPTER TWO

LOVE

"This is my commandment, that ye love one another.
As I have loved you."

John 15:12

Divine Love is the only kind of Love that can be expressed self-lessly. Only this real Love can heal all things. It is how God Loves His children—everywhere, always. And it is the kind of Love I am called to express toward my neighbour. The more I practice this commandment, the more sense it makes. I now understand that this has very little to do with the human emotion we often call *Love*. That old concept of Love is very limiting, but the new view of seeing each other as possessing all the qualities of God includes every good that can be realised. This is how we are to Love.

To truly Love anyone, I must first Love myself. And to Love myself is to know my true identity as the image and likeness of God—the very expression of Truth and Love. When this understanding is firmly rooted in consciousness, I am able to recognise that same Truth in others. Romans 13:10 makes this clear: "Love worketh no ill to his neighbour: therefore, Love is the fulfilling of the law."

This deeper Love is unselfish—Love in action. It is being willing to act in a way that uplifts another, or to think thoughts that bless and heal. It is loving because God is Love, and His image must express what He is. This unselfish Love is the kind Jesus exemplified. It does not condemn, nor does it condone error. Rather, it Loves enough to correct false thinking and wrongdoing—offering the courage to help those who are willing to be transformed.

Only Divine Love can heal, for only Divine Love has the power to separate evil from God's child. The more I keep Love in my heart, the more naturally it expresses itself—and with it comes the strength and courage to meet every challenge. This is not an intellectual exercise. I know that all God's children are flawless, regardless of the material evidence. But expressing this Love comes with spiritual demands. It asks us to surrender pride, self-justification, self-love, self-righteousness, and self-will. We cannot express Divine Love while harbouring any form of negativity.

I find it challenging in some situations, but I have also experienced the deeper joy and fulfilment that comes when I am able to put such Love into practice—the results are worth it.

Loving one another blesses us all. I was praying early one morning about an inharmonious family situation. It became clear to me that I should include everyone in my prayers and see each one as God's perfect child. When it came to certain members of my family, however, I felt a resistance to seeing them as good and perfect, possessing all of God's qualities. I found myself focusing instead on their wrong habits—such as drinking and dishonesty—rather than releasing such thoughts entirely. I knew I needed to humbly ask for God's help in seeing them as His children, in obedience to His law.

I had to relinquish the stubborn belief that these family members were somehow separate from God, that they did not reflect all the good that God is in Truth. As I struggled to move past this mindset, a thought came to me—as if someone had asked, "Would you be forgiving of those who are unyielding in their racial prejudice?"

This comparison hit home. It became so clear to me that I was no different from those who hold on to their prejudices. Any attempt to see others as imperfect is an offense against God's supremacy. It is like saying I do not believe my Father is perfect or that He has created spiritually perfect children.

If I were unwilling to forgive prejudice in others, could I honestly expect to be forgiven when I refused to see any of God's children as perfect spiritual beings? Whether or not they chose to behave rightly did not make them any less than what God knew them to be. I asked myself if I really believed God had created drinking, dishonest children. The answer was no. So, I knew I had to release such thoughts entirely.

I continue to pray to obey Jesus's commandment to Love one another. I insist on completely exalting the idea of a perfect God— and therefore the "spiritual beings" God created as perfect, too. My responsibility is to do God's will, and that has brought me peace. I know that continuing to see these family members rightly is itself a blessing, and that this helps to free them from those bad habits, rather than reinforcing such behaviour as part of their true being.

Jesus warned about wrongdoing and showed the right way because He Loved deeply. This kind of Love enabled Him to never accept the evil of sickness as accurate about anyone. In my work, I strive to Love like this—to feel this Love—so that I may be of genuine use to those I am led to help. What good is a selfish Love that ignores wrongdoing? Or a self-righteousness that condemns another?

It is easy to be kind to others—doing good deeds to fulfil a latent need for approval or popularity. But the true test of Love's strength is our ability to forgive and forget when someone has deeply wronged us. When we are offended, we are called to address the wrong, continuing to recognize the person's authentic selfhood. This kind of Love measures our loyalty to God. Jesus forgave every wrong—that is our example.

We cannot truly Love while still criticizing or attaching wrongdoing to someone's character. "Beloved, if God so loved us, we ought also to Love one another" (1 John 4 11). When our thoughts are preoccupied with judgment or resentment toward others, we close ourselves off to receiving holy thoughts about ourselves.

As we rise higher in thought about everyone, we become more attuned to the spiritual sense that guards us from danger and temptation. When we Love this way, we gain increased spiritual insight—discernment to know what to trust and when to be cautious in our relationships. In doing so, we release every part of our lives into His hands and seek to let Him lead us.

When I read about individuals from different African tribes who, after committing atrocities against one another, are still able to come together in reconciliation—or when I reflect on the Bible story in Genesis 33:4, where Jacob and Esau embrace after Jacob had sorely offended his brother—or when I consider prisoners who, after years of wrongful imprisonment, choose to forgive—I realise that only the power of God's Love can enable such forgiveness.

This forgetting of hurt in order to see someone rightly requires a power beyond human capacity. The greatest example of such Divine unselfish Love is Jesus's forgiveness of those who crucified Him. Could anyone, by human strength alone, Love that much?

Only the healing grace of God's dear Love, welcomed into our consciousness, can vanquish hatred. Then—and then only—can we experience the freedom to be the expression of Love. It is impossible to harbour hateful thoughts and still express genuine Love.

Matthew 5:43-48 advises us to Love differently; we are told to Love our enemies because God Loves everyone—the just and the unjust, those who do right and those who do wrong. As His children, we must do the same.

Proverbs 11:18 states, "... to him that soweth righteousness shall be a sure reward." If we allow ourselves to be used by Truth to express the nature of God—which is only good—we can expect to have happier experiences. In my healing ministry, I have found that I cannot pray for healing unless I keep Love in my heart. Truth will heal, but it does not dwell where any form of hate is present. These incompatible vices include irritation, resentment, and indifference, all of which are forms of hate.

The Bible tells us in Matthew 4:1-2 that when Jesus was tempted, He had fasted for forty days. He had been seeking closeness with the Father; hence, when the evil suggestions came, they found nothing in Him. He was able to rebuke them immediately. In my own experience, the more I keep thinking rightly—focusing on the things of God—the more quickly I can detect wrong suggestions and reject them as having no place in me.

Proverbs 16:3 helps me in my effort to keep my thoughts clean: "Commit thy works unto the Lord, and thy thoughts shall be established." Another verse, James 1:13-14, reinforces what tempts us:

"Let no man say when he is tempted, I am tempted of God: for God cannot be tempted with evil, neither tempteth he any man: But every man is tempted, when he is drawn away of his lust, and enticed."

Jesus's Love healed because it did not seek to satisfy what the material senses were claiming. Love for God was enough. It recognized sufferers as the image and likeness of God. That kind of Love is what heals. It is the kind of Love that beholds the perfect spiritual being so clearly it "unsees" blindness, leprosy, lameness, immorality, and even death as realities. Steadfast Love can restore the true man of God's creation.

Some of the good we claim to do is not truly good. We must examine our motives for rushing around doing "good." If we are constantly bailing people out because we want to be perceived of as kind, they may lose the opportunity to give up destructive habits.

Here is an example. Consider a man who spends money foolishly and is always in debt. In such a case, what good will another financial endowment do? We would help him far more by lovingly showing him that the false sense of pleasure in his habit is not truly part of him, as an idea of God. If we hold him in our thoughts as a man possessing the qualities of discipline, a sound Mind, and orderliness, he may be more fully blessed—if he is ready to be.

This is why it is so important to ask God for His loving guidance always. Then we will know when to do and when to do it, and our actions will become genuinely loving—and truly blessed.

This may sound impractical, but let me ask you: Are there times when you feel Love impelling you to act on someone's behalf? And are there other times when you feel compelled to act simply because it seems to be your duty?

A friend of mine was in the hospital once, and he said that most of the people who came to see him seemed more interested in how badly he had been hurt than in how he was doing. He said he could tell they did not come out of genuine caring—because after their curiosity was satisfied, not one of them came back.

It is also unhelpful to rush to someone in distress with the thought, *Oh, poor so-and-so.* Jesus consistently saw the perfect spiritual being in every situation. Because of this ideal reference point, He had the power to heal. Perhaps we, too, can learn to see one another rightly, while providing for practical needs as we feel led.

Our obedience to loving in this way would bless all. I once observed something that brought this Truth home to me. I was going through orientation to become a volunteer at a shelter. The orienteer repeatedly emphasized that we had to be mentally stable ourselves in order to work in the facility, alluding to disturbing situations that sometimes arose. It was clear that many people had been coming there for years. The director, though very dedicated and loving, seemed extremely busy and pressured.

It was apparent to me that the director was a Christian, and I felt sure she prayed before coming to work. But I was puzzled: if she had faith in God, why did she appear so burdened? Why did she continually refer to how busy she was? Truly living a Christian life, I thought, should help her overcome this false sense of pressure that was disturbing her harmony.

I no longer believe my Life should feel pressured. If it does, then there is something more I need to understand about my relationship with God. The only "worthwhile" pressure, I think, is the Divine impulse to draw nearer to God. It is a feeling I recognize when I have allowed my thoughts to drift into wrong-thinking—a clear sign to return quickly to the sacred place of right consciousness.

We must go about our daily lives with a peaceful recognition of who we are. God is our centre, and there is no disturbance there. I overcame the fear of having too much to do by cultivating spiritual poise—gained from the knowledge I can do all things through Christ who strengthens me (Philippians 4:13). This helped me move through my daily responsibilities with complete surrender to Christ, trusting Him to work through me in all that needed to be done.

One day on my walk, a thought came to me: Shouldn't our Love be bigger than our houses? Shouldn't our Love be larger than anything we possess? Our hearts should be so filled with Love for ourselves and everyone else that we bring this Love wherever we go.

If we believe in Love and Harmony, we will experience Love and Harmony. I cannot think badly about others, accept the wrong they do as being part of their nature, and still experience good in my relationships with them. I have found this practice to be especially important at work. There is power in good; hence, justice is superior to injustice, and forgiveness is more powerful than resentment or anger. These are the predominant realities that will replace any negative lies. Every false belief I entertain—even briefly—not only harms me but also darkens the veil that blocks all humanity from seeing the goodness we should be experiencing.

This awakening translates into my daily Life in refreshing ways. When false suggestions come in the form of excuses—trying to dissuade me from reading my Bible lesson—I remember why I need to read every morning before my day begins. The most persuasive reason is that my preparation of thought each morning has an extraordinary impact on all my daily affairs.

The consistent practice of starting my day with God helps me to expect good in all I do, in whatever way God chooses to supply the need. This way of thinking shapes all my interactions with the people I meet. It influences how I think; I seem to have a calmer sense of where I am to be and what I am to do. Even more rewarding is the realisation that my correct thinking blesses mankind by clearing, if only slightly, the mist of false beliefs which enslave us all—rich or poor, black, white, or yellow.

Any wrong thought anywhere in the world impacts the multitude of false beliefs we have been taught to accept as true. We must all strive to overthrow the tyranny of these beliefs. Our collective freedom will come not from anything external, but from the power of individual and shared right thinking—for that is what determines our experiences and actions. So, before you give in to slothful suggestions or excuses that would prevent you from doing your part, think of the impact of your work—and what an immense effect it would have if we all did ours.

In the past, offensive behaviour tormented me because I condemned the wrongdoer. I now recognise such attitudes as evidence of a lie—an error in belief about who we truly are. In every wrong experience, someone has been hoodwinked into believing they are capable of the behaviour they displayed.

I know now that in all such experiences, we must respond in a way that fosters lasting healing. Whether we speak or remain silent, we must prayerfully listen for the Truth that will replace our wrong thoughts. If we do this, we remove those thoughts, and their effect are vanquished—or at least diminished. In doing so, we strengthen our place in this worldwide army to overthrow evil in all its forms.

One day, two people thanked me for talking to them. One was a lady who asked a question when she entered the store. No one answered her, so I did. She thanked me and added, "People don't talk to each other anymore." The shop helper should have responded—it was clear she had heard the question. What thought, I wondered, might have held her back from simply being polite to a customer?

Later that day, a woman walking beside me on the street said, "I am so tired! My feet hurt." She was wearing a pair of comfortable Reebok sneakers, so I asked, "Even in those shoes?" She proceeded to say that she had just finished forty minutes on the treadmill and was now walking over ten blocks home. When we parted, she also thanked me for talking to her.

We do not know what people are going through. I believe that sometimes it is not the answer one is looking for—it is the feeling of being seen and acknowledged by another human being.

And this makes me wonder: Why do we feel lonely when Jesus has always promised the Comforter's presence. " . . . lo, I am with you always, even unto the end of the world." (Matthew 28:20). We should strive to be more in tune with what others are experiencing—to be alert to whether we should say something or simply affirm the Truth silently for our brother or sister.

If you love God, then you know all people are capable of loving, and our purity remains intact as a reflection of God. Try this: one morning, set everything else aside and think only of God.

When we give, we must examine our motives and the effects of our giving. I have come to understand that the greatest good we can do for another is not merely to give materially, but to help each person recognise the good they already possess. We should give in order to demonstrate the abundance available to all.

We should forgive—and be blessed. You have heard the saying, *Forgive and forget.* If you truly forgive, you will forget the wrong, because only good is real. Do you often hear someone say, "I'll forgive, but I won't forget"? Why bother to forgive if you are still clinging to the harm that was done? You do no one any good unless you do both.

The person who is forgiven also has a responsibility. We do not forgive so that the person may go on and repeat the offense. For forgiveness to be complete, there must be reformation on the part of the one forgiven. This reformation confirms the healing that has taken place, as it shows that someone has let go of the belief that the wrong action is a part of who they are. However, we cannot feel responsible for another's continued wrongdoing. Once we have cleared our own thoughts about someone and feel at peace with the situation, we have done our part.

Evil has a way of reminding us of the bad things that have happened in our lives, but we are given authority from God to choose which thoughts we will accept. Who can we blame for that? We must not dwell on bad experiences.

Only good comes from God. So-called bad experiences are not from God. This was difficult to grasp as long as I continued to believe that what my senses told me was real. Bad experiences are all part of the material dream. They never change my spiritual perfection, and like all dreams, they can fade—if I do not continue to remind myself of them. Whatever was bad will leave my experience if I no longer accept it as real in my consciousness. Since God is Spirit, spiritual reality is all.

All our relationships—especially at work—require the demonstration of spiritual qualities for them to survive. Consider the relationship between police and the public, lawyers and their clients, doctors and patients, parents and children, accountants and clients, doctors and nurses, administrators and employees, retailers and customers, or politicians and constituents. The harmony and sustainability of these relationships depend on the qualities we bring to them. This proves that honesty, dependability, justice, kindness, respect, honour, and integrity are all superior determinants in how we relate to one another. We are far more likely to return to a place of service—or work again with someone—when those qualities have been demonstrated.

Maintaining a loving relationship with people you do not live with can be very difficult. I used to say I could tolerate them for eight hours and then go home, but I soon realised the bad thoughts I had about co-workers did not stay at work. I carried that mist with me, which clouded my ability to see as the Father sees. Sooner or later, something else would arise that I would perceive wrongly, and *voila!*—wrong thinking would continue as wrong feeling.

However, when I allow justice, love, health, unselfishness, and forgiveness to dwell constantly in my thoughts, their opposites eventually disappear. That is why it is said that when we point one finger at someone, at least three will point back. The thinker of wrong suffers more from the effects of their own wrong thoughts.

John 10:16 states, " . . . there shall be one fold and one shepherd." This Bible promise reminds me that we are all one, under the same supreme government. During the recent financial crisis, it became clear how interconnected the world truly is. What happens in Washington, Wall Street, and America's main streets affects events on their European equivalents, which in turn influence what happens in so-called developing countries.

Philippians 2:4-5 says, "Look not every man on his own things, but every man also on the things of others. Let this Mind be in you, which was also in Christ Jesus;" These verses are calling for us to love one another. They echo the great commandment: to love our neighbour as ourselves.

Galatians 3:28 states, "There is neither Jew nor Greek, there is neither bond nor free, there is neither male nor female: for ye are all one in Christ Jesus."

Psalm 133:1 says, "Behold, how good and how pleasant it is for brethren to dwell together in unity!" We are reminded many times through Scripture of the importance of unity.

I have come to think of unity not only in terms of organisations, but also as the mental recognition that all people are one in our shared expression of the qualities that belong to God. We do not have to contribute to charitable organisations in order to effectively support goodwill toward mankind. If our regular thoughts are aligned with good, we accomplish much.

One of my friends once said they loved themselves—and their faults, too. I did not quite understand what she meant. If faults were good, they would not be called faults. A fault is a weakness in character, an imperfection. It does not sound like something we should love or want to keep. I used to think of faults as something to be proud of, as if they made me tougher. I thought it meant one was tough. However, now the desire to associate myself with such imperfection has gone away.

Scripture tells us in Colossians 3:9-10: "Lie not one to another, seeing that ye have put off the old man with his deeds; and have put on the new man, which is renewed in knowledge after the image of him that created him." We also read about the psalmist's desire to be cleansed of his secret faults in Psalms 19:12. ". . . cleanse thou me from secret faults."

Sometimes, if a fault appears to offer some benefit, we tend to hold on to it. But what benefit can a fault truly bring? Since it is a fault, it cannot help us in any way—nor can it help those in our lives. The more I set my affections on loving and pleasing God, the more I lose the false sense of myself.

Another example is whether to react with fear or to remain calm when things seem grim. It could be fear of a worsening illness or financial lack that appears to overwhelm us. Here, too, we are called to stay calm and stand our ground with the Truth of God's infinite provision for every need. When we realise that we have never moved away from God, and that His inexhaustible ideas are ready to supply all that we need, we can respond appropriately. God may not answer in the way we think He should, but we can trust that His answer will be the best one in the long run.

I cannot neglect to tell you how difficult it was for me to keep my focus on God while the bills were piling up. But I realise now that I held the wrong balance between good and so-called evil.

I must watch my motives for the good I do. I often ask myself whether an action serves my ego in any way. At times, there is a latent desire to be thought of as good; worse still, sometimes my motivation is pity for the so-called victim. But the good I do must be inspired and directed by God. In this way, it is not self-serving, but an expression of the realisation that all good is of God. He works through me to glorify His name.

God could not create what is good and allow some other power to destroy it. Therefore, it is only in a dream—or in mistaken beliefs—that anything bad appears to be real. To believe that wrong or evil is part of us is to deny the omnipotence, omnipresence, and omniscience of God.

In recent disasters—earthquakes and floods—some have asked whether God could have sent such calamities. What we see is limited to what our human view can comprehend. Because we live at this level of understanding, these events appear painful and sorrowful. We struggle to see beyond the veil of human perception—to the perfection that still exists intact, even as bodies are being removed.

Unselfish Love kept Jesus's thoughts forever aligned with Truth. He was able to see every negative circumstance as non-existent in the perfect realm of Spirit. Even at the crucifixion, Jesus remained conscious of the power of a present God. That ability to be steadfast with the Truth of God's only-ness enabled Him to Love unselfishly—to see the true selfhood of those who crucified Him and to pardon them.

If Jesus, because of His suffering, had accepted the cruelty of those tormenting Him as part of their authentic selves, and had become angry or disturbed, He would have been admitting the existence of another power apart from God.

This same unselfish Love can help me see other ills as unreal. Even a broken-down car can seem like an affront to God's ever-present power. All wrong or difficult circumstances cast a shadow or tell a lie about the Truth of right mobility, reliability, comfort, and the ability to be where we are needed.

One day, my husband was on his way to work when the water hose in his car burst. He was able to bring the car to a safe place, and I drove him to work. He had the hose repaired for a very reasonable price. But several days later, the same thing happened—this time at a different location on his way to work.

He was led to drive to a nearby town, where he saw some truck drivers and asked them for help. They directed him to drive to a town about nineteen miles away, where he found an auto-part shop for help.

After asking five people, my husband was about to give up when, finally, the sixth man inquired about the problem. That man happened to have a mechanic friend. He called his friend to see if his friend could help—only to find out that, at that very moment, the friend was already at the auto parts shop all the truck drivers were recommending.

This driver was able to describe the issue to his friend, who then purchased the necessary part. He came and repaired the car—again, at a nominal fee—which enabled my husband to get to work. My husband later described the whole incident as funny, and it led him to make some new friends.

Unless I separate any form of sin from the person, I cannot move forward in forgiveness. This has been very difficult, because at first, I simply could not separate someone's wrongdoing from their Christly self. However, this higher sense of Love deals with jealousy, envy, hatred, resentment, and other such vices. God's child can only reflect higher qualities—honesty, harmony, satisfaction, and contentment. This understanding makes it easier to separate those vices from myself and from others. It has been the greatest test of how much I truly love.

Any wrong committed robs someone—whether of their peace, their Trust, or something they need—working against the spiritual fact of God's allness and our perfection. Such actions imply that the wrongdoer believes in their own incompleteness, which motivates their behaviour.

But without a person to attach them to, jealousy, greed, envy, anger, hatred, and pride lose their reality and their power. Can any of those qualities have an effect unless they are believed to belong to someone—someone who believes they are jealous, envious, hateful, proud, or angry?

What kind of Love do I have? Is it the kind that is willing to sacrifice what my mortal senses are seeing and rise higher in thought to the kind of Love Jesus expressed? This higher, unselfish Love is the kind that prompted God to give His only begotten Son, that we might have Life. This Love—referred to as *agape*—does not identify another person with sickness, dishonesty, or any evil quality. Instead, it defies the testimony of the mortal senses in order to rescue that person from the evil trying to wear their face.

This Love acts to provide comfort or to speak to wrongdoing in a way that awakens another, but it does not hold the evil or wrong as the person's real being. In this way, a person's pure nature is separated from the counterfeit picture of evil, be it sickness or any other vice. We must never forget that we are all God's children.

We are called to Love everyone by seeing them rightly—not only those with obvious challenges, but the true selfhood of every individual. Even the best-dressed or wealthiest person could be facing unseen, aggressive challenges.

This kind of Love is inherent in all God's children and should be expressed. When I think of my earlier work as a nurse, I reflect on its deeper meaning. The dictionary defines the verb *nurse* as to nurture, cherish, care for, or mend. To me, it simply means to love enough to take some action that helps restore what is broken to its wholeness.

Such action might take many forms. It could be a smile that reassures someone that all will be well, a bowl of soup offered in a moment of need, or a kind word that lifts someone out of sadness. We can all express that kind of tenderness—and we all need it.

We begin by being nurses to ourselves: by recognising our own wholeness, and by cherishing and nurturing that wholeness as children of God. From there, we can nurse our family members, our neighbours, our co-workers, or anyone we might meet in the course of our day.

These nursing qualities can then be expressed in our homes, our communities, our towns, cities, or villages—and certainly in our countries and throughout the world. Just imagine the impact it could have if we all thought of ourselves as nurses.

In essence, we are all nurses. So let us get to work.

This kind of loving is the most potent weapon we have against anything, because it expresses God, and nothing is mightier than the power of God.

Let us see what insights we will gain from our next chapter on **MARRIAGE AND HOME.**

CHAPTER THREE

MARRIAGE AND HOME

"What therefore God hath joined together, let not man put asunder."

Matthew 19:6

There can be more harmony in a marriage when you think of your husband or wife as a child of God. The right understanding of who we are influences the qualities we bring to a harmonious marriage.

The Bible says, "What God has put together let no man put asunder" (Matthew 19:6). It does not say, "What has been put together by someone's personal wish." Since God is the one doing the relating, He will also do the maintaining—if we continue to seek His counsel and obey it.

I once saw a humorous message on a billboard that read, "God said, 'Loved the wedding, invite me to the marriage.'" We must put God first in our marriage and seek divine guidance in everything we do after the wedding ceremony.

It may appear that every marriage begins because two people are "in Love." But the phrase *in Love* carries a deep meaning. If two people are truly in Love, then—since God is Love—they are, in a sense, *in God.*

Still, we often take this for granted. If a man and a woman are in Love, they are acknowledging that their source is found in God. Therefore, they should also accept that they are the embodiment of all that is good. They are not separate from Him, and so they have the capacity to express every Godlike quality they each possess.

Since marriage is good and godly, a couple already possesses the wisdom they need to honour the responsibilities and commitment that contribute to a harmonious union. They can enhance each other's spiritual growth. They should sustain one another with encouragement and remind each other of the Truth when self-doubt creeps in.

Anyone who has experienced married life must confess it is not always easy, and at times, it can feel downright wretched. Wisdom in choosing a partner is vital. Marriage is one of the most important decisions we will ever make. And who better to guide that decision than God, the all-knowing Mind?

Yet this is often the very choice we insist on making ourselves. We assume our Love for the other person is enough to determine our course. But we must pause and consider the responsibilities and obligations that come with marriage. Our own will can mislead us. We may be tempted to prioritise physical beauty, income, profession, or even the admirable qualities mentioned in chapter one. But truly, only God knows, and we should rely on Him to lead us in this most significant decision.

Pretending to love someone is a grave injustice, and it sometimes happens sometimes out of fear. Selfishness leads to many divorces.

What is interesting is how often we believe the *other* person is the selfish one. Yet selfishness—rooted in self-love, self-justification, and self-righteousness—is destructive in any relationship. It blinds us to the true selfhood that reflects God's likeness. Would a reflection of God not care whether another's needs are met? Could indifference be part of God's expression? Surely not. No one would try to dominate another if they understood that every expression of God is worthy of respect, kindness, and love.

It is equally horrifying to think that husbands can be jealous of their wives' success, and wives can envy their husbands' achievements. The saying that behind every successful man is a good woman is true, but it is equally true that behind a successful woman must be a good man. *Good* contains the godlike qualities that comprise both male and female attributes: strength, wisdom, justice, orderliness, and firmness for men; and love, kindness, gentleness, comfort, and encouragement for women.

Because we are complete reflections of God, we manifest both His female and male attributes. This makes the idea of spousal jealousy seem entirely unreasonable. My husband's achievements must be welcomed with praise and gratitude, for they are manifestations of my own awareness of male qualities, which I possess as well. In the same way, a wife's accomplishments must reflect the man's awareness of his womanhood.

We all have the innate tendency to want to help. We see evidence of this in how people respond to disasters. Successful marriages make happier homes; happier homes make happier communities, towns, and counties. Happier communities make happier nations, and a happier world.

When I realised what a precious idea marriage was, I also began to learn lessons about my own. Affection dies when it is not nurtured, when indifference and complacency replace active interest. I have learned never to see myself or my husband as less than what God made us.

If we allow God to do the relating in the first place, then when challenges come, we will know they are opportunities to prove God's governing presence. We both can appreciate His Love for us and our sincerity in obeying His laws. We also remain committed to being grateful for the great gift of our union.

I must not allow my mind to dictate any negatives about my husband. When I am not careful, waves of negativity cloud my thoughts, overshadowing the pleasant qualities I should be focusing on. I must claim more of the spiritual attributes of my husband, rather than sabotaging my own prayers by daily affirming the very faults I do not want to see in him.

God, my Father–Mother, is my health-giver, life-giver, lawyer, employer, business partner, husband, wife—my everything. We do many unloving things and yet still expect good. I used to ask my husband or son to do something, while deep down expecting that either they wouldn't do it, or they would take forever. After thinking this way, I would act disappointed when indeed they failed to do what I asked or delayed in doing it. Then I would ignorantly excuse myself from the outcome and feel sorry for myself. I condemned them, attaching wrong behaviour to who they are.

We must anchor our union on the foundation of spiritual Truth. When we both know our union with God, we cherish our relationship as an expression of that great gift. We know then where to turn to gain lasting answers to our challenges. We can both promote unselfish Love and care for each other. We can give honest compliments freely and receive them humbly, with gratitude. There is no need to belittle each other or to feel superior.

Finding ourselves in God becomes a spiritual viewpoint that allows for the expression of the following qualities: respect, humility, patience, forgiveness, selflessness, and spiritual strength.

These qualities replace all the others that culture, religion, and the world assign to us. Then we can see each other only as the manifestation of the individual God created. It is wrong to use culture or religious laws of any kind to continue to subject, dominate, or take away someone's freedom.

Home is universally important. I marvel at how even birds and ants show great interest in whatever constitutes their home. We all know some of the familiar phrases that highlight the significance of home: *Home is where the heart is . . . Home sweet home . . . A man's house is his castle . . . You can have a house and not a home . . . Charity begins at home.* The ability to exercise charity at home translates into charitableness in our experiences outside the home. If I cannot be kind at home, I will not know how to be kind anywhere else.

One day, my daughter looked at me and said, "Mummy, I don't remember when our house looked so beautiful." The only thing I could think of was gratitude—for my regenerated concept of home, now embodying warmth and peace. Home is far more than a house or a physical place.

I once heard a man who had been a foster child speak very emotionally about being moved from home to home, and how it still affected him. This new sense of home could possibly help such individuals to begin healing the deep hurt over not having a place to live.

At the same programme, I heard foster parents speak. It was heart-warming to hear one of the women say that in order to adopt children of different racial backgrounds, you must truly know who you are. Her husband did not initially know how he could love the adopted child because of her race. He prayed about this feeling, and the result was that he and the child now share a very special bond. Love shows us who we are, and Love can transcend the skin colour, reaching deeper to the Truth about each of us.

I commend kind-hearted foster parents for reaching forth with the Love of God to care for others. We all possess that genuine goodness within us, and children respond to Love that validates who they truly are. Their talents emerge, and they begin to perform at the level of their inherent good.

Those considering this noble endeavour should pray and let God make the connection. Stereotypes about teenagers or older children can interfere with decisions about whom to adopt. However, if prospective adoptive or foster parents trust what the Scriptures say about humanity, there would be more positive placements.

The potential outcomes are beautiful: so-called problem children on medication becoming straight-A students with a future. The unconditional Love that lifts them into the awareness of who they really are makes the difference. Foster or adoptive parents can help children move beyond their histories and embrace a Love that sees no wrong.

A home is a dwelling place, but if you think about it, what makes a home, a home is the feelings we associate with it. Home is identified with comfort, security, beauty, warmth, joy, and all lovely qualities. In that light, a hut can be a better home than a mansion.

Let me share an illustration. I was watching a documentary on public television many years ago, in which a film crew was interviewing a man in a village in Niger, Africa. It was dusk, and the whole village looked calm under the setting sun. The film crew went to the man's hut, and he lit his lantern. I do not know why, but there was something very remarkable about his home—so much so that I still feel compelled to write about it all these years later.

His bed was a simple wooden frame, a few inches off the floor. He had a pillow and a piece of cloth laid across it. There was not much in the room, but it was orderly and serene.

What I cannot forget is the absolute peace in that simple space. The interviewer asked him if he was ever afraid. "No, I am not afraid because I know God," he replied. His answer reflected an unshaken understanding of his relationship with God.

What this man had is available equally to all if we seek it. Home is spiritual—because we are spiritual beings, only our spiritual view of home is real.

Since I am a reflection of God, my true dwelling place is in that perfect, pure, and safe consciousness of God. This may sound ethereal, but it is also deeply comforting. Spiritual realities become practical; the acceptance of spiritual truths about home brings about change in the home.

And since home, too, is also a reflection of God, then home must be perfect. The Bible has much to say about the qualities of home. 2 Corinthians 5:6 and 1 Timothy 5:4 teach that the home is associated with harmony, security, sufficiency, and permanence. Therefore, it is protected from violation. Wherever I may be, I am never separated from the qualities of comfort, security, harmony, and peace. I never lack a real home. It is this awareness of what my true home is that prevents the feelings called homelessness and homesickness.

The home, which is an idea of God, cannot be disturbed. It is the dwelling place of the King of Peace and Love. Lawlessness and disorder cannot be part of this expression of God, nor can disunity, friction from stubborn human will, contention, or strife of any kind.

I know with confidence that God maintains and protects the home. Where there seemed to be a need for repair in my own marriage, I met this with the knowledge of God's ability to supply my need. Since perfection cannot coexist with imperfection, I know that every seeming need was just that: a seeming need.

God's laws are supreme. They will vanquish any intruding conditions that tend to cause discord and will restore whatever is necessary to bring about conditions that are in keeping with His laws of Peace and Love.

Many sayings tell us about the significance of a home: *Home is where the heart is. A house is not a home.* I like both sayings. The former speaks to the qualities of peace, rest, joy, love, and tranquillity. The latter further emphasizes the importance of the non-tangible concept of home.

A nice house is not necessarily a good home. When we talk of a broken home, we are not referring to the physical structure. A broken home is the disruption of the harmony, Love, and Peace that give a home its true meaning.

We learn throughout the Scriptures that our home is in God. "Come unto me all ye that labour . . . and I will give thee rest" (Matthew 11:28). Heaven is our true home. Only in God do we find all the qualities that truly make a home, those everlasting qualities mentioned above.

If we love God, we should strive to live according to Jesus's teachings. The greatest prayer He taught mankind begins with "Our Father." This prayer unifies humanity and points to our common source. The admonition is "love one another," not "love only those you live with in your physical home."

In obedience to the Scriptures, we must embrace the idea of family as encompassing all humanity, with one God as our Father–Mother source. All good comes from God, who is our real home. We must continually bathe our consciousness in honesty, Love, compassion, thoughtfulness, and harmony. Such consciousness is one with God, and this is the family home we will experience, for "as a man thinketh in his heart, so is he:" (Proverbs 23:7).

Our real family includes all mankind. Thus, our true family home can only exist in pure consciousness, where we experience God through those loving qualities that warm our hearts and make us feel loved. He gives us a sense of security, provides ideas that meet our needs, and grants us peaceful rest. This is the family home, the only home where we can truly rest.

A friend once described home using the acronym "Harmony of Mind Expressed." Home, for me, is my divine consciousness, the place where God dwells. Therefore, I must keep it clean and protect its integrity by shutting out all that would disturb or spoil this sacred place. In Ghana, some refer to this inner housekeeping as "cleaning one's home." A harmonious mental atmosphere naturally expresses itself as a happy home.

Now, when I travel, instead of worrying about what my daughter might be doing, how my husband's work trip is unfolding, or how my dog is managing, I replace those anxieties with the realisation that God is all. God is everywhere, and each member of my family is always an expression of God, no matter where they are. They remain secure in His loving embrace, protected and firm in Truth and Love.

This knowledge brings me profound peace. It has the spiritual power of Truth, dispelling the fears that might otherwise cloud my mind. Other forms of fear could also unsettle me: doubt, worry, suspicion, guilt, self-pity, or self-righteousness. I acknowledge that I cannot be everywhere, nor can I be responsible for everyone. It is wiser, then, to trust fully in God's supremacy and omnipresence. When I hold onto this Truth, I can no longer be fooled by anxiety's false promises.

In Sunday school, I learned Hymn 849 from the Methodist hymn book. Back then, it didn't mean much to me, but now it holds a profound meaning for my daily walk with our omnipresent God:

> *Father lead me day by day,*
> *Ever in thine own sweet way,*
> *Teach me to be pure and true,*
> *Show me what I ought to do."*

This hymn has now become an expression of Truth that occupies my every thought. The Spiritual essence of home is with me wherever I go. My faithful adherence to my identity as a child of God, and to the infinite allness of God, frees me from anything unlike Him.

We must reach out to give to the homeless and comfort the homesick, because these actions demonstrate God's ever-present Love for all His children. In doing so, we affirm that the recipient is a beloved child of God who is never truly lacking. They are simply receiving some of the abundant good with which God continuously blesses His children.

Jesus clearly demonstrated the true idea of home. He said, "The Son of man hath not where to lay his head." (Matthew 8:20). Yet look at all He did for mankind; wherever He was, He remained in the presence of God and thus embodied every quality that constituted the true sense of home.

People came to Him to be fed, and He fed them. He healed those who came seeking healing, and in His presence, they experienced comfort and peace. Where previously there had been condemnation, they left feeling worthy. He restored life where there had been death, and health where there had been sickness. He brought harmony to the frightened and unhappy, constantly reassuring and encouraging them. He knew God to be the true home for all mankind, and He was filled with an everlasting abundance of everything God's children could ever need.

Let me share how this new concept of home helped me. Several years ago, we had to sell our business, and I moved to another state to begin a career in the healing ministry. It was not an easy transition. Many days and nights during those initial months away from home, I frequently found myself in tears. I felt deeply saddened that I had left Atlanta and was separated from my family.

You can see how wrong suggestions work. There I was, blessed with many opportunities for higher education and spiritual growth, yet unable to recall any of the good. Instead, I focused completely on the lie that my life had become a rollercoaster of disappointment and failure. Soon, self-doubt set in, convincing me I was responsible for the failure of our business. When I received the direction to restructure the business, I did not have the courage to see it through. I had allowed myself to be overwhelmed by discouragement.

Through all this, I never stopped reading and yearning to understand God better. I wanted to be obedient to what He desired for my life. One day, it became clear that I needed to study more deeply the idea of home. The realisation that I was always at home in the presence of God reassured me. The qualities of comfort, beauty, peace, and harmony were present right where I was, even if this was a single room.

The awful feelings of regret and self-doubt faded, leaving me uplifted. This experience also helped me to realise what was most important. God's plan was in operation, and at the right time, if it were His will that I return home, I would. Not long after this, I distinctly felt that it was indeed time to move back home. A new work opportunity arose, and the entire transition was filled with quiet joy. Had I not moved, I would never have grown to accept this spiritual concept of *home*.

When I awakened to these spiritual Truths, I recognised that God supplies the loving ideas we can use to express beauty and comfort in our homes. I received simple, inexpensive ideas that helped transform the appearance of my home. With a modest budget, I purchased beautiful tiles, dried flowers, and other decorative items, which have brought a warm atmosphere to our den.

Our understanding of *family* stems from a deeper, more loving comprehension of the Lord's Prayer. Jesus prayed, "Our Father," something we cannot take for granted. Malachi 2:10 reminds us that we all have one Father. The prophet Isaiah declared, "... thou O Lord art our father, our redeemer" (Isaiah 63:16). It is equally comforting to read about God as our Mother. Isaiah also said, "For thus said the Lord ... As one whom his mother comforteth, so will I comfort you" (Isaiah 66:12-13).

I am a child of God; when I feel selfish, I must replace selfishness with selflessness. When I am vengeful, I must choose forgiveness. Psalm 119:165 assures us, "Great peace have they which love thy law: and nothing shall offend them." My obedience to forgive prevents hurt feelings that might otherwise last for years, and it spares me the painful disturbance of losing my peace.

God is the loving Father-Mother, the real parent of all families, and the head of our households. Just imagine a family in which every member knows their true home is in the presence of God. Imagine further that each child understands their household cannot contain negativity, so even the children strive willingly to obey the rules of their Father–Mother parent.

I try to apply this understanding to my family, and the results are wonderful. No matter what challenge arises, I know my duty is to affirm the Truth that God oversees the household and maintains its perfection. Then, by listening, I discern the appropriate human steps to take, always expecting good results.

Family members provide us with opportunities to view the world correctly: how wives view husbands and how husbands view wives, how parents view children, and how children view parents.

One thing that helped restore greater harmony in my marriage was choosing to listen to God for His direction on how to respond to any seeming wrong. I learned that my approach must be loving. The power of Love is far stronger than any method I could devise to solve the problem. Now, instead of reacting angrily and only then turning to God, I turn immediately to Him, expectantly listening for guidance on how I should view and handle the situation.

I had previously tried the approach of my attempting to change someone. It never worked for long and often led to a self-righteous attitude, which could be offensive to the person I was attempting to correct. A far more effective method was to let God handle it. God is speaking to each one of us, and He is heard when we listen to Him. The power of His Truth resolves whatever discord might be present.

We *must* correct wrong traits, habits, and behaviours in our children and in each other. In prayer, we can seek courage, as well as the right way and the appropriate moment to rebuke what is ungodly. This must always be done with the motive to bless.

Here is an example. I have changed how I respond to my husband leaving our kitchen in total disarray after cooking, replacing anger and frustration with calmness. Instead, I pray for the best time and the right words to address what needs correcting. I also pray to continue to see him rightly and to trust that he can see me rightly too. Approaching these situations in this way has brought more peaceful solutions. Knowing that all the members of my household can express orderliness and beauty has helped make these qualities real in our home.

I have often been surprised by marriages of twenty or thirty years ending in divorce. I used to wonder what could have saved such marriages, believing that if two people could no longer find satisfaction together, it was perhaps better for them to go their separate ways. Now, however, I realise that viewing each person as God's image can indeed save marriages. Conversely, if marriages continue with each partner emphasizing the faults of the other, the result is inevitably divorce.

We can shift our perspective of each other by recognising the qualities of God as everyone's true nature. Seeing one's husband or wife correctly restores good and harmonious thoughts and feelings and can save a marriage. Right thoughts become our reality.

It appears that a high level of disappointment often leads to the problems that result in divorce. Clearly, we feel disappointed when we do not receive something we expected. How much responsibility are we placing on each other for our happiness in a relationship? To what extent are we relying on marriage for fulfilment, or expecting it to guarantee our joy? What formed the basis of the marriage? How deeply have we truly loved our partners?

Viewing everything in our lives from a spiritual standpoint places it on a firmer foundation, and marriage is no exception. Our real union is with the Father, and nothing can separate that union. Everything we need is included in this relationship with God, and the purity, innocence, and joy of that spiritual union can be expressed in our marriages.

Let us see what insights we will gain from our next chapter on **EDUCATION.**

CHAPTER FOUR

EDUCATION

"But the Comforter, which is the Holy Ghost, whom the Father will send in my name, shall teach you all things . . . ."

John 14:26

D o you sometimes wonder why, despite the advanced education possessed by the world's leaders, there appear to be no answers to our woes? International summits alone cannot help people achieve good health or escape poverty and hunger. We have overlooked something vital in our education: the role of divine intelligence.

When I was in elementary school, my mother advised me to approach every test with the knowledge of this verse from Exodus 25:22: "And there I will meet with thee, and I will commune with thee from above the mercy seat." I recall with gratitude this insight about God's ever-presence. Her advice helped me remain calm and perform to the best of my ability. This shows that God is the source of our intelligence and cannot be excluded, even from our academic work.

Let me share a wonderful experience that illustrates this point. I was about eleven years old, preparing to move on to secondary school the following year. I needed to travel for an interview at the school I would be attending. At that time, none of my siblings were home, and my father had travelled to another town.

My mother was unwell, and I had to travel alone the next day for this important interview. I went to the market and bought ingredients to make soup for my mother. After finishing all my tasks, I sat with her and had her ask me questions from a book we thought might be covered in the interview. After some time, my mother chose a story from Aesop's Fables, about the woodcutter and his axe. I read the story, answered her questions, and then went to sleep.

The next day, I travelled about sixty miles by bus to my future school. On the way, I reflected upon some of the Bible verses my mother had often used to encourage us, and I felt reassured by God's presence. I arrived at about nine in the morning. It was a sunny day, which lifted my mood. My interview started promptly at 9:30.

During the interview, I felt calm, partly because my future headmistress was very pleasant and had a warm, loving smile. However, I was not sure how well I was doing. Then, for the last part of the interview, she handed me a story from Aesop's Fables to read for about thirty minutes, after which she would return with questions. I could hardly believe it when I saw that, out of all the stories in that book, the one given to me was the exact same story I had read the previous night. Needless to say, I was able to answer her questions clearly. I could hardly wait to get home and tell my mother what had happened. She was delighted and gave thanks to God. I was accepted into the school and did very well there.

I am certain we all have experiences like this one that prove God's guidance, yet we often forget His ever-presence. Can we really afford to leave God out of our education and behave as though *we* are the source of our intelligence? There is nothing we need to know that we cannot learn if we turn to Him for answers. Understanding this Truth breaks down the barriers, suggesting that those from particular backgrounds cannot succeed in certain subjects.

We should not make children feel limited in any way. Thoughts like *Oh well, math or physics are difficult* should be abolished. We can replace such thinking with the knowledge that, as long as our thoughts reflect God's divine intelligence, there is nothing we should know that we cannot know.

We cannot be satisfied with an education system that does not bring True freedom. Should not one of the tests of educational success be the extent of one's moral growth? Our willingness to do what is right demonstrates our closeness to God. The Love of good should be emphasized as part of every curriculum. We teach the practice of hygiene from an early age, along with the consequences of neglecting it. It is heartbreaking, then, that children are not taught how deeply they can rely on the Truth of their birthright as children of God.

In 1 John 1:5, we read, "... God is light, and in him is no darkness at all." This light is intelligence, wisdom, and correct thinking. Even Jesus knew that all wisdom comes from this Great Light. Therefore, if we receive a bright idea, the glory belongs to God and not to us. This realisation calls for our humility.

Our system lacks spiritual education—an understanding of our higher nature. In this purer consciousness, impurity of any kind becomes intolerable because purity and impurity cannot coexist. Only in our right consciousness can we know our true identity as reflections of God and recognise that everyone else shares the same identity. With this understanding, we would no longer call others names or attach false attributes to them simply because they are different. God made all; therefore, there is good everywhere.

It is clear that even a high academic degree from the best school, on its own, cannot prevent us from being greedy, unfaithful, fearful, envious, jealous, or angry. This reveals that another kind of education is needed—one that will inform and influence our academic enlightenment and help us to realise our spiritual completeness. How often are truly brilliant young people incarcerated, sometimes never to return to society, simply because they were never taught how to handle the temptations of lust, anger, jealousy, envy, greed, and hatred?

Not all of us dream of becoming president. Those who are chosen to lead a nation should have God's call. But I am certain that we all please God when we do His will. It is not the attainment of education or high office that matters most, but how our spiritual education helps us to realise who we truly are. As we read in Ecclesiastes 12:13, "Let us hear the conclusion of the whole matter: Fear God, and keep his commandments: for this is the whole duty of man." Ultimately, it is doing God's will that brings true freedom.

This is not to belittle formal education, but there is no record of Jesus receiving one. Yet, His unwavering understanding of who He was made Him the greatest man who ever lived. He said we can all do what He had done if we believe in Him. He did not say we could do these things with a degree in Theology. He knew that right thinking is something everyone can choose. Thus, our impartial Father-Mother God has made the most important things available to all.

It is clear that a PhD does not necessarily come with a degree of right consciousness. The many examples of poor conduct and judgment among those who attended the finest institutions confirm that academic achievement alone does not teach righteousness. In fact, such achievements can often mislead people into believing they are self-made. They begin to identify with their accomplishments, developing a false sense of pride and self-righteousness, which can be accompanied by a dangerously inflated self-concept.

When I was growing up, my father used to say, "We cannot write ten ahead of nine." It is a proverb that signifies the importance of order-liness. It is essential to do things in the proper order. Otherwise, we make mistakes. We must be willing to wait patiently and allow the orderly plan for our lives to unfold as God reveals it. Sometimes we rush ahead of God's plan.

We cannot insist on writing ten before nine and expect the right solutions to our challenges. Can anyone truly convince the children of a poverty-stricken village to leave their farms and attend school, only to graduate and find they have no jobs? What, then, would be the value of their academic sacrifice?

We leave much undone when we fail to teach children how to listen to the still, small voice that comforts, enlightens, and leads in every circumstance. If we did this, our children would have the true foundation for all necessary education. This is shown in the outcomes of formal education. While today's economic system tells us that academic education is the only path to a good job, it does not complete who we are, nor does it free us from life's deeper troubles. How can we ignore our moral education and spiritual growth when so many of our experiences depend on them? As parents, it should matter most to us that our children understand the power of prayer.

We often hear in the news of prominent men who fall from their high positions and suffer complete humiliation, losing everything, because they never learned the truly important things in Life that could have helped them master the appetites that led to their ruin.

What would cause a preacher to overcome the temptation to go after prostitutes? What would lead a policymaker to create unselfish laws that benefit all? What would stop employers from being unfair and unjust in all they implement? What would keep a president from thinking he should amass wealth only for his own family, forgetting the true requirements of the office he holds?

What makes a wife consistently loving, yet not feel unappreciated for the loving things she does? What keeps an employee committed to giving their all to the opportunity they are given, demonstrating the best of their talents in order to be a blessing?

The answer to all this lies in an educated consciousness. At any time, it is what we think that will translate into our actions. If the thought is repulsive to an enlightened consciousness, then the right action cannot follow. We do what is right because it is consistent with who we are.

It is interesting to observe how some people feel so important because of the degree they hold. Yet many with less academic education come up with some of the best ideas to benefit mankind. This confirms that we should all look to the Father for our ideas. "In all thy ways acknowledge him, and he shall direct thy paths" (Proverbs 3:6).

When we have a good idea, we should never believe that we somehow originated it. Our true worth has little to do with the degree we have earned. A degree should never substitute for your real identity. The ability to remain humble, regardless of which school we attended, is a saving grace. Many who graduate from the so-called "best" schools make the school their identity and expect certain advantages, which may lead to major lifetime mistakes.

Academic excellence does not equate to excellence in what matters most: obedience to God. It is clear that obtaining a high academic degree does not guarantee a sustainable path in life. Otherwise, we would not have so many people with doctorate degrees working in jobs unrelated to their education or having to settle for positions that are far less sophisticated.

A degree in morality should be the highest degree one can achieve. We do not need a formal classroom for that, and we do not have to pay any fees to obtain it. When we see religious leaders committing social crimes, we wonder what they missed in their education. In times of temptation, nothing is as effective as a consciousness that has outgrown sin.

Remedial programs have high levels of recidivism. These programmes overemphasize academic achievement while neglecting to educate the consciousness, so individuals no longer tolerate wrong thinking and wrongdoing.

Public schools require children to engage in a great deal of physical activity. One reason for this may be to help them stay out of trouble. But children also enjoy reading and having meaningful discussions with adults, if they are taught early on that one of the most important exercises is to think about good things.

We should teach children that it is all right to want to be alone sometimes and just think. They should feel comfortable in their own company, with their own thoughts. Those moments can become some of the most precious when one feels God's nearness. If we developed this habit in childhood, it would be easier to continue it into adulthood. It would be as natural as brushing our teeth. The first thought we should turn to is God. He is our very Life.

It should not be only adults who read our holy books. We should make them something desirable. If we are reading them often ourselves, children will learn that this is something they ought to do.

Education should be the responsibility of each of us because we are all setting examples every day. In our efforts to make children better achievers, we cannot neglect what is most important. As often as we make ensure they achieving high grades in mathematics, English, and science, we should also be asking how they are doing with honesty, right thinking, handling anger, frustration, irritation, self-doubt, discouragement, and negative thoughts.

The excuse that we are human and not perfect is often used to defend certain actions. We all falter, but we should not be comfortable identifying ourselves with habits we know are wrong. That is like admitting we are helpless in our tendency to do the wrong thing. It was disheartening to hear some youth in remedial school describe themselves by the labels they have been given—anger management, sexual misconduct—the very vices that brought them there.

We cannot allow these qualities to grow unchecked. We can prevent the falsity of uncontrolled appetite by teaching the importance of balance and moderation. We can overcome some of these habits if we are taught our true identity and that we have God's power to enable us in our victory.

You never know who is watching your reaction to something. The way you respond may teach someone a better way. Children notice everything. I am amazed at the incidents my children recall from their early years, and how vividly they narrate certain moments, making sure I know what they learned from them.

Children do not have to think that improving consciousness is only for Sundays. If our goal is to uplift our consciousness, what better time to start than from childhood? Unfortunately, we often teach our children to fear. I remember that when we were growing up, we were constantly reminded how difficult adulthood would be. Grown-ups would say, "Wait till you grow up," implying that hardship was waiting for us in the future. Such warnings are often given in an effort to get children to behave appropriately. But a child might reason, *if the hardship is in the future, why should I do the right thing now?*

When we work hard and study hard, there is often a sense of pride in the achievement, as if it were accomplished through human will alone. But all good comes from God. We must have the humility to recognise that it is God who has done it, and we must give Him the glory. Even Jesus never took credit for the good he did.

There is a need to teach children this. We must teach them not to believe that mere human will, pride in self, or positive thinking brings success. True success is measured by how one aligns with God's plan for His child. When something great is accomplished that blesses many, it is always the triumph of Truth, humility, honesty, patience, persistence, and the fear of God.

We should also teach children to Love being good, to cultivate good thoughts, and to act rightly for its own sake—not simply for the promise of a car or a vacation. Using our God-given talents honours God and is our sure way of thanking Him for His mercy and for allowing us to be His children.

It will be a beautiful day when moral sophistication becomes the most important measure of success, instead of academic achievement. Our need for Christliness should surpass every other need. Nothing else can bring the Peace that this realisation reveals.

We should be careful not to promote the use of human will, which completely shuts out the presence of an all-powerful God. I am concerned when I hear children voicing self-reliance and trust in human achievement as the most important vehicle to satisfaction. However, my heart is warmed when a young child learns a happy attitude because he grew up seeing his father's example. Contentment is a part of our nature.

Our understanding of who we are, always in the presence of God, is the only perfect Principle that can guide us through all of life's tests. We should not mislead children into thinking they are only successful if they become a lawyer or a doctor. Their real success is determined by whether they are shining in the purpose God has placed them here to fulfil. Any right work can bless if one's moral character is strong.

All good work blesses humanity. The fact that many presidents are lawyers does not make law the only honourable profession. After all, we can have only one president at a time, and even he needs to eat and have a home cleaned. There is a need for cooks and cleaners, whose work should never be looked down upon. They are equally important in making the "whole" complete. Such roles, when held with confidence and honour, bring joy and satisfaction to those who do them.

I once had a painter come to my apartment, and by the time he left, I was convinced that he was the very definition of success. He told me the story of how he came to America as a child. Although he and his family faced hardships, he was full of gratitude for all that God had given him. He had so much joy, and it was obvious that he loved to paint. He did it with great expertise. You could see the Love in his work. His children were all doing well in their professions. He was also deeply caring in his community and church.

I will never forget his broad smile, which expressed gratitude and Love for his work and Life. Someone may think that being a painter is not much of an achievement, but that man was as successful as they come. He had enough academic knowledge to do his given work. The qualities he expressed brought him everything he could possibly need. It was clear that what he did was not just a job. To him, it was far more than a mere source of income.

We err when we try to solve a problem with mistaken principles. Children from lower economic backgrounds or broken homes should not be labelled as *at-risk*. The moment we begin with that negative labelling, we sentence ourselves to imperfect results. The correct principle, once again, is to see every child as God sees them—perfect and pure, reflecting the intelligence of God, their true Parent.

We must pay attention to how we think. In doing so, we will fall into the error of assuming people from different cultures are incapable of certain tasks. We are all from the same Father. Nor should we assume that the child of a single parent will inevitably perform at an at-risk level. That is a double error. First, it suggests that the absence of a human husband in the home must result in certain deficiencies. But what of the promise: "For thy Maker is thine husband" (Isaiah 54:5). If the so-called single mother embraced this Truth about herself—and if others thought of her this way too—we would see very different results. To truly help our neighbours, we must begin with right thoughts about them.

It is heartbreaking to hear of those who fall victim to their passions or to emotions they were never taught to outgrow. This happens to all kinds of people: educated, uneducated, and even the highly educated. The FBI estimates that the number of teenagers being groomed, trained, and forced into prostitution in different cities across the country increases every year. Crimes involving sexual exploitation are prevalent.

This troubling trend reveals the urgent need to educate people to raise their consciousness that is grounded in self-worth. We need an education that helps us master the brutal and animalistic instincts. We need the recognition that there is a common enemy—one that must be exposed and vanquished. The enemy is incorrect self-knowledge.

Education that enlightens consciousness will lead to self-government, which can reveal our true heritage as children of God. It is clear that more attention needs to be paid to what we are teaching children to believe about their genuine selfhood. Once a child understands that they are the reflection of God, and they are taught what that means, they are not likely to forget it, just as one plus one equals two is never forgotten once it is understood.

This understanding forms a far better foundation from which to draw the moral strength and moral courage that are part of our inheritance as the spiritual children of God.

Let us see what insights we can gain from our next chapter on **FEAR.**

CHAPTER FIVE

FEAR

"There is no fear in love; but perfect love casteth out fear:"

1John 4:18

Anxiety, worry, apprehension, fretfulness, frustration, and doubt are all forms of fear. I often wonder how I could have ever broken free from these if I had relied on pills to manage them. What lasting good would any pill have done? If I keep wiping up a pool of water without repairing the leak itself, I will be wiping forever. Similarly, the underlying thoughts that give rise to anxiety, worry, and frustration must be addressed if anyone is to be truly free from fear. Simply calming someone with medication or other therapies may offer temporary relief, but it cannot bring lasting Peace.

What freed me from the stubborn grip of fear was a clearer understanding of who I am. It does not make sense that, all over the world, fear is tolerated—when in Truth, it should not be accepted at all.

Yet when it appears, we often accept it as real without question. This enslaving lie continues to imprison us, whether we are behind physical bars or caught within our own mental strongholds. In one way or another, fear, anxiety, worry, and depression shape how we think and act.

Fear can present itself as worry, anxiety, hate, pride, deceit, pain, and sometimes as physical symptoms. You may recognise in the list below some of the thoughts or beliefs that cause uneasiness of Mind:

- Fear of sickness and pain
- Fear of not having money, a job, or income
- Fear of humiliation
- Fear of feeling pressured or being late
- Fear of being criticized
- Fear of feeling dominated
- Fear of injustice
- Fear of discrimination
- Fear of feeling unloved or of loneliness
- Fear of losing fame or popularity
- Fear of looking stupid
- Fear of failing
- Fear of the unknown
- Fear of someone taking our positions or our personal property
- Fear of being who we really are
- Fear of being afraid

Jesus knew that fear is torment; hence His endless admonition to resist it, as in, "FEAR NOT, little flock; for it is your Father's good pleasure to give you the kingdom" (Luke 12:32). After such a list of all that encumbers our lives, one may wonder: what is left to live for?

It is important to know exactly what we are afraid of. When a sense of fear begins to build in any situation, we should ask ourselves: *What prevailing belief is making me afraid? What false sense am I accepting?*

The Bible warns against tolerating the serpent—symbolic of fear and deception—and teaches that neglecting to confront it keeps us subjected to its claim. This lesson is powerfully illustrated in Exodus 4:2-4, when Moses was commanded to face what he feared: "And the LORD said unto him, What is that in thine hand? And he said, A rod. And he said, Cast it on the ground. And he cast it on the ground, and it became a serpent, and Moses fled from before it. And the LORD said unto Moses, Put forth thine hand, and take it by the tail. And he put forth his hand, and caught it, and it became a rod in his hand."

Fear can almost paralyse us. Yet remember, after this experience, Moses found courage. In obedience to God's command, he led the people out of Egypt. His words to the children of Israel reveal great strength and unwavering trust in God: "Fear ye not, stand still, and see the salvation of the Lord" (Ex. 14:13). Having overcome his fears, he was now clear about the power and presence of God.

The Bible holds answers to all these fears. The word of God offers lasting freedom if we are willing to receive and obey it. What is remarkable, even paradoxical, is how we often seek divine help, yet resist the very thoughts and actions that would bring us into the light.

One day, I received an email from a gentleman who sounded desperate with fear. The subject line was in bold letters: "PLEASE

HELP ME." His message was full of painful memories, reaching as far back as his childhood. Now, in his mid-sixties, he described his life as having been nothing but pure hell. He had struggled to maintain relationships and admitted to bad habits, including drinking and smoking. Then he went on to condemn himself for the pain he believed he had caused others.

He listed numerous physical complaints and shared that none of the many doctors he had seen were able to help. He said his father had always put him down. Altogether, it was a tragic account of a man who had accepted a false identity. He was suffering from self-misidentification. What he was truly seeking was the light—the Truth—that would show him his real selfhood.

As long as this man continued to believe all these things, he had no chance of seeing the Love of God, which is the true reality always at hand. And what he was doing is not so different from what I once did, or what many of us might admit we still do.

In the latter part of his email, he asked me to pray for him, saying he was "prayed out."Many people had already prayed for him, he said, but he still found no relief. He said he could not change his thoughts. He had been praying day and night for God to send the Holy Ghost to heal him. However, he gave no evidence of true repentance; instead, he insisted that he could not stop smoking or give up other bad habits.

Here was a man who was crying out for help—yet placing more faith in the evil he was experiencing than in the good he could experience. It seems our faith and trust have, in some cases, been relegated to "evil believing", and this misplaced faith can be so tenacious that we cling to it, even as we cry out for help. But if we were to shout our sounding "Not True!" to every lie, every wrong that appears in our experience, we would begin to align ourselves more fully with the power of good.

In Ps. 19:12, we read, "... cleanse thou me from secret faults." Are not these secret faults—envy, jealousy, covetousness, pride, resentment, impatience, lust, doubt, depression, desperation, despondency—like hidden mists that prevent us from seeing our real selves as the reflections of God? These faults occupy our thoughts and, in doing so, become idols that usurp Christ's rightful place in our thoughts.

All people are subject to God. Therefore, the misuse of power, whether at work, in marriage, at school, at home, or between parents and children, is wrong. Similarly, using age, culture, or illness as excuses to manipulate others is also a misuse of power.

Wrong thoughts create fear. Psalm 34:4 says, "I sought the Lord and he heard me and delivered me from all my fears." Just as in physics, where friction arises from opposing forces, there is a spiritual tension when humans will oppose God's will. This resistance breeds anxiety, fear, and restlessness. We may feel anxious when we feel we should be somewhere before the right time, or when we long for something that we are meant to wait for. I have felt this anxiety myself, especially when I knew I should be doing one thing but chose another out of wilfulness.

Yet if we yield entirely, letting go of our human opinions and turning fully to God with trust, His will unfolds. Divine wisdom brings peaceful answers to our questions.

Look at how much of the old thinking is preventing this dear gentleman from seeing the Love God is pouring his way. It reminds me of how my own focus on all the negatives once kept me from taking even the first step toward realising peace. It has taken time and intentional effort to release those false concepts. But obedience to the call to replace the old with the new—be it slow or fast—is the only path to healing.

Fear can be conquered through humility, which makes room for the Love of God to be felt. It may seem unusual to speak of humility in the context of fear, but true humility has nothing to do with feeling inferior, submitting to injustice, or lacking the courage to stand up for what is right. Rather, humility—in its proper sense—confers strength and courage because it brings the awareness of our oneness with the only power there is.

Humility is the quiet strength that can declare, "I can do all things through Christ who strengthens me" (Philippians 4:13), acknowledging our unity with God and the power that conveys. This is quite different from a kind of humility that accepts inferiority or separateness from God. That kind of false humility often masks a subtle pride—a pride in a self apart from God. And wherever that pride exists, fear soon follows.

Jesus's example is one we are called to follow. He demonstrated that the Spirit of God was with Him in every moment, and He continually acknowledged that it was the Spirit accomplishing the good He was doing. As John 6:63 says, "It is the spirit that quickeneth; the flesh profiteth nothing:" And in 1 Peter 5:6-7 we are reminded, "Humble yourselves therefore under the mighty hand of God . . . for He careth for you."

When I appreciated that Jesus was never afraid, and the Bible consistently warns us about fear, I saw clearly how I had mistaken timidity, which is fear, for humility. Our humility should arise from a deep gratitude for the realisation that we are children of God. It is the recognition that everyone else is also a child of God, and that God has no favourites.

Poor childhoods and difficult life circumstances should not be the reason we are humble, for those experiences were never true of our real being. God's children are all royalty—we just do not realise this. When we are timid, we are afraid, and we are separated from God in belief; for where fear is, there is no Love. Timidity reveals our trust in fear and our distrust in God's power, here and now.

To realise myself as perfect in God's great Love required me to let go of fearful thoughts and take hold of a renewed consciousness of Love. I had to know that I am loved, that I am lovable, and that I am loving. This renewal of thought has not been easy for me to experience. I have not only had to affirm these loving Truths for myself, but I must also continue to affirm them as the true nature of all.

Can you imagine having to love someone who has always been unkind, who gossips about you, and envies you? This is the kind of striving that practical Christianity calls for. Human goodness is commendable to a point, but we must look to Christ Jesus's teaching. He understood that fear is nothing in the presence of God's love.

Fear of punishment alone never truly corrects anything because it merely breeds dishonesty if it is not replaced with Love. When someone refrains from wrongdoing out of fear of consequences, it does not mean they will not commit the act again. The desire remains in thought and will surface again when that desire outweighs the fear of punishment.

At other times, we may stop a particular action for selfish reasons, not because we find the action repulsive in our consciousness. There is an element of dishonesty, for example, when children refrain from stealing simply because their father is at home, only to steal when he is away. What we need is a consciousness that says at all times: *stealing is not a part of me. I cannot steal because I am a perfect image of God.*

Each time I accept a fearful thought as real and dwell on it, even for a moment, I dishonour God—because for that moment, I am declaring that there is no God. Yet if God is all, then good is always everywhere. This allness cannot be denied. Love, therefore, must occupy its rightful place in my consciousness.

People can overcome their fears through self-will, but that kind of courage cannot compare with the insurmountable power of Love. Fearlessness that is not grounded in the courage of Love can still succumb to evil. We see this in the varying degrees of fear, depending on material circumstances. For instance, many people experience less fear when they lose their jobs than when they receive a grim medical prognosis.

My mental banner says: *Stop! God Is All. He Occupies All Space; There Is None Beside Him.* This helps me immediately check any discord and dismiss it, allowing me to focus on what *is* true about my Life in any given moment. It helps me remain vigilant in casual conversations, lest I absorb false beliefs I should have outgrown. Pressure, anxiety, stress, decision-making, injustice, failure, disappointment, pride—and all forms of fear—succumb to the power of Love and cease to be real in my consciousness when I remember this mental banner.

Consider *The Song of Solomon* 2:4: "He brought me to the banqueting house, and his banner over me was love." God's Love is an infinite healing balm, always present to calm and heal every false sense of fear.

One morning, as I woke, I heard this: "Do not be afraid when you have taken a stand for Truth, nothing can happen when Christ is in control. Go higher when the tempest rages; this is the only way you can prove the omnipotence, omnipresence, omniscience, and omni-action of God." You can imagine what great comfort those words brought me.

Always remember: the discord that seems to frighten you is only an illusion. It is erasable, and you have the divine presence to wipe it out. Seeing discord in this light did not happen overnight. It has taken persistent prayer to understand and Love God, and to gain this new way of accepting situations. The Truth we need to replace any discord never changes. These Truths are forever available for us to use.

One fear I had to learn to constantly refute is the fear of not having enough money. I persist in this because it has often dissuaded me from going forward with some of Love's wonderful provisions for supplying my needs. After we pray for supply, do we sometimes freeze, paralysed by the fear of lacking money, right when an idea has come? I certainly did this when we were on the verge of giving up our store.

At the time, I had been focused on how we would add food service to the store and how such a plan might be implemented. Because I did not see the money in the bank, nor did I know how we were going to raise that kind of money, I simply worried about the entire idea. I also assumed my husband would not support the project, given our past unsuccessful attempts to raise funds for store improvements.

Through prayer, I was led to a local university that was developing a programme to help small businesses expand. When I went there, the programme director was very encouraging and showed genuine interest in what I was planning. However, she referred me to another woman who was to be my adviser. That meeting was disheartening. The woman seemed unfriendly, even angry, and she offered no encouragement at all. When I left her office, I was overwhelmed with discouragement. Every wrong thought about the idea not working came rushing in. I felt so exhausted and defeated that I convinced myself that my husband would not see how the plan could succeed. And so, I gave up the idea entirely, without trying to explain it to him.

I was wrong to be fearful when God was leading me. There are examples in Exodus 25-28, where God gave precise instructions on how the ark and the tabernacle were to be built. And in Genesis 6, Noah was given the exact specifications for building the ark, including the type of wood to use. These examples teach me that when God gives an idea, the details of how, when, and where are also included. They should not be doubted.

In my case, fear was magnified, and I disregarded the gentle guidance to go forward with something that would have blessed many. This was disobedience to the power of God. From that experience, I learned several important lessons. First, to always hold fast to my true identity, and to acknowledge the correct identity of everyone else. This would have given me the courage I needed and the spiritual perception to see through the fear that was being presented. Second, I would have seen the adviser rightly, perceiving her real identity instead of what was presented as an angry woman. Third, I would not have made the judgment that my husband would fail to see the feasibility of the project. And fourth, the most significant lesson was to make everything I do about God. What God ordains cannot help but bless everyone involved. The when, how, and why of God-given ideas are always His responsibility, not ours.

The only confidence that truly benefits us is grounded in the Truth that God is the only power, presence, and source of all knowledge and right action, and that He is in control at all times. This is the solid foundation of confidence worth trusting. It is sure, with guaranteed certitude of help in every need.

In Ephesians 4:22-23, we read, "That ye put off concerning the former conversation the old man, which is corrupt according to deceitful lusts; and be renewed in the spirit of your mind." We are to do this *now*. Some of the calls I have received were from parents speaking about what their children will or will not do. As we spoke, the conversation often revealed a lingering, wrong thought about the child, based on something the child did in the past. How do we insist on attributing wrong qualities to God's children and still expect different outcomes in our experience? I continue to be watchful not to criticize, judge, or condemn anyone. When I catch myself entertaining such thoughts, I quickly reverse them with the truth.

One area where fear tempts us most is in situations of injustice, whether at work or at home. The fear of losing a job or the false security of home becomes magnified. In those moments, it can feel difficult to know what the right thing is to do. But these are precisely the times when we must express patience—not as passive waiting, but as quietly and faithfully reaching for God's answer regarding the next step. God's goodness is the present fact of our lives. Adherence to this Truth can give us the spiritual uplift to wait for the unfolding of God's will, with full expectation of a positive outcome.

When we wait, we do not wait because of our own human will, someone else's opinion, or even because some ridiculous church creed says so. We wait to hear God's direction, because there is no mistake there. I used to say I could not hear God. I blocked out His voice with negatives, with distrust in His power and faith in doom, self-pity, fear, discouragement, and despair. We cannot perceive God's loving guidance, because we will not find Him where fear claims to be.

I am sure most of us have failed enough times in things we have done out of fear to know that if we do anything motivated by fear, we will fail. As long as the premise is wrong, we guarantee ourselves failure.

As I witness the power of God and how it operates in our lives, if we let it, it becomes clearer that leaders, parents, and teachers all need more trust in the unfailing presence of God. Such trust urges us to seek His help more readily, and to use His guidance in our affairs. What are we doing with the good God has given us? 2 Timothy1:7 reads, "For God hath not given us the spirit of fear; but of power and of love, and of a sound Mind." Power, Love, and a sound Mind are all everlasting qualities, given directly by God, for our liberty.

*Let us see what insights we can gain from our next chapter on **A JOB, A BUSINESS, OR A CALLING?***

CHAPTER SIX

A JOB, A BUSINESS, OR A CALLING?

In Paul's words,
" . . . it is God which worketh in you both to will
and to do of his good pleasure"
Phil. 2:13

We are God's work; therefore, we possess strength, joy, harmony, order, and wisdom, and we are perfect as reflections of God. Think of yourself as the work of God—complete, flawlessly maintained, and loved by Him. The only thing that needs changing is our own thinking.

With this in Mind, I now see work from a completely different perspective. Work is my "right activity," and I therefore hold it in higher esteem. From the spiritual viewpoint, this means I am always in the right place. I am complete, so I am inseparable from right activity. This affirms God's care for me; He leads me to make the right adjustments that allow for the fullest use of my potential, talents, and godlike qualities to bless others.

These insights lead me to admire those who are genuinely happy in their work. It suggests they are in their right place, using their talents to bless mankind. Such people are not working out of selfish motives, nor are they at a particular job merely because it offers health insurance or other benefits.

In the acknowledgment of our completeness, we can expect our right work to be part of us. Expectation of good is right thinking; it comes from recognising ourselves as God's children. Only good can come when our prayers are sincere. Therefore, I cannot pray and then anticipate doom. Psalm 58:11 says, " . . . Verily there is a reward for the righteous: verily he is a God that judgeth in the earth."

Right identification of who we are helps define our work experience. When there is dissatisfaction at work, what is your first question? Is your first thought, *I can leave*? A co-worker once said, "I got here looking, and I can leave looking for something else." But is that really the answer? Do you pause to consider that you are truly in God's employ? It is often more right to stay and bless in the best way possible, while praying for the assurance that you are where God wants you to be. The right answers always come—though not always immediately.

Another scriptural Truth that has helped me overcome the suggestion that I could be unfairly used by anyone is found in Luke 10:7: "the labourer is worthy of his hire." We must use the talents we have been given. Success is more readily attained when our steps are directed by God, and inspired accomplishments bring a more lasting joy than any born of self-will. A plan laid out with divine direction makes our human steps orderly. I have also found that, even when the task at hand seems daunting, there is an unseen power that buoys my strength all the way to harmonious accomplishment. It is helpful to affirm for yourself that only God can use you.

All the right ideas for work come from God. He could never conceive of an incomplete idea, so whatever work is to be implemented is already being carried out according to His way. It makes no sense to try to figure out on my own how I am to do it. Since God gave the idea to begin with, it follows that I should seek from the same all-knowing source how it is to be fulfilled.

How sincerely we surrender all to God has a real impact on every area of our experience. I once spoke to a friend who had been in the same job for nearly forty years. She had clearly outgrown the role but lacked the courage to seek change. You may feel the same way about your job—it is no longer fulfilling, there is no joy, and you go through the motions. Perhaps you have come to believe the job is your only source of income. I used to think that too—even while saying, like many Christians, that God was my source.

I do not mean to suggest you should quit your job without having a deep and convincing trust in where your source lies. Instead, begin to associate the word *infinite* with the good that God is. If you need an opportunity to use your talents, know that there are infinite opportunities, and you will be led to the one that is yours. There is a boundless means of supply for everyone.

Prayer and listening will inspire us towards right thinking and right action. We must strive to elevate our thoughts by knowing these Truths until they become as natural to us as 1+1=2. No one who understands that simple mathematical fact can be convinced otherwise. In the same way, when our doubts and fears have subsided, we begin to see clearly what the divine outcome is—and the work is completed in His perfect way.

I believed more in the power of the bills than in the incomparable might of Truth and Love to supply whatever I needed. I now know that my faith in good must always be stronger.

I am grateful for my work because it gives me an opportunity to use my talents. After eleven years of doing practically the same thing, I became fed up. I knew I would be leaving the following year, but how I was going to continue doing a good job in the meantime felt like a real problem. Through my study, I learned that thanking God is a remedy for every problem. I began to reflect on why I did the work I did, and I became sincerely grateful for the privilege of sharing God's loving care.

Once I began doing that, I experienced the greatest satisfaction I had ever felt in my work as a medical nurse. I felt more fulfilled than I had during all the previous years in that profession. This experience proved the power of gratitude.

Cultivating an attitude of expecting good, along with the acknowledgment of God's infinite supply, is especially important in business. I came to understand this lesson much later, after our family business was sold. Looking back, I can see many moments when I would have benefited from that spiritual insight.

Now I understand how important it is to recognise that business is an idea from God. If it is the right business, thinking of it as God's idea keeps it within God's care. With that premise, one can more easily apply the law of harmony to business. You can think of your business as already complete, lacking nothing needed for its successful fulfilment. I apply this insight to my work today. Interestingly, I still feel some of the same doubts and disappointments—but not nearly as often, and not nearly as deeply. These feelings are quickly dispelled when I pause and recognise that I am dealing with an idea already made perfect in God.

I feel a sense of calm when I take a moment to realise that everyone I must speak with or meet is also God's child. I know I am providing something they need, and therefore, there will be mutual blessings. That understanding has given me the courage to do the work I am meant to do.

My understanding of business began to take shape when I was pondering the passage in the Bible where Jesus said to his disciples, "Cast the net on the right side of the ship, and ye shall find." When they obeyed this instruction, "now they were not able to draw it for the multitude of fishes" (John 21:6).

This Bible story has offered me valuable insight. The disciples had toiled all night and caught nothing. That image of toiling at night signified, for me, the confusion and disorder of a darkened consciousness. Yet in the morning, the light of Christ replaced the darkness, and at Jesus' instruction, multitudes of fish were caught. They had not changed their location—but they had changed their view at Christ's command, and they saw the superabundance of what they had been seeking was already present.

At a time when I could not balance my business cheque book and was experiencing frequent overdrafts, I lacked the spiritual understanding to see those financial struggles as impositions upon God's unlimited bounty, which is, and always has been, my true substance. I did not reason that, because of my correct identity, I could not lack, and neither could my business. Instead, I accepted the lie of limitation until I felt engulfed by the fear of overdrawing—and that is exactly what happened.

I had to recognise that I possess the Mind of Christ, which cannot be mesmerized into believing in any sense of lack. Simply thinking positively is never enough because I could just as easily begin thinking negatively. It is only through the purity of divine Mind that the correct view of any situation can be gained. When I realised that, as a child of God, I could only possess the Mind of Christ, I began to see the present spiritual perfection of my finances—right where lack had seemed to be.

The third important lesson I have learned about any right activity is to know, at all times, that God is in the midst of it. "The LORD thy God in the midst of thee is mighty; he will save, he will rejoice over thee with joy" (Zephaniah 3:17). Enthusiasm in any right endeavour is essential; it reflects the benefits of acknowledging God's presence in all our work.

One morning, when I went to the bank to make a deposit, I noticed one of the tellers seemed rushed—in both his manner and appearance. His words reflected this: "Monday is always a killer, it's so busy, it doesn't let up." He kept making such comments as he counted the notes handed to him. I wondered what calm he might have felt if he had paused for just a moment to realise God was in the midst of all his activities.

Have you ever been reluctant to leave a job or close a business you knew was running its course, but continued anyway? Often, I believe we do know when it is time to move on. However, we get caught up in human reasoning—telling ourselves we should stay. Sometimes we are afraid to leave because of health insurance or the comfort of a steady income. And yet, it is interesting how many people, after being let go, go on to do work that is more meaningful, more rewarding, and far more satisfying.

Sometimes, we are meant to be used in another place. Our talents are meant to bless elsewhere. This Truth has helped me deeply appreciate the verse, "all things work together for good to them that love God" (Romans 8:28).

In my own case, when I left the place where I had worked for twelve years, I knew I was meant to move on to something different. Yet I took another job out of fear and a desire to do something I was familiar with. It felt safer. But that sense of safety did not last. It was the only job I have ever been fired from. The position was a night shift, and I was tired of working nights. I never lacked compassion for my patients, but the long commute and other circumstances made it clear that the job was a poor fit.

At that time, I was not fully relying on God's direction. I did not trust enough. I did a great deal of human planning and figuring out. So I stayed, even though deep down, I knew I should leave. When the owner called to discuss my departure, I knew it was the right decision. She did not cite anything I had done wrong—she simply said she wanted one of the other nurses to take my place. But I understood. I felt so relieved that I did not even experience the usual panic over when the next pay cheque would come. I had only been there about six months, the shortest duration of any job I have ever had.

That transition led me to be more diligent in my spiritual study and brought insights that have truly changed my life. What may have seemed like a failure at the time ended up bringing the greatest reward.

Today, I think of work or business as a right activity. I am only interested in worthy endeavours—not those that simply make me money, but those that genuinely bless my universal brotherhood: my community, my country, and the world. In a network marketing venture I once joined, I listened to many of the high earners talk about what brought them true joy. After buying the cars, the homes, and the vacations, it was the impact they had on others, the help they were able to offer, that brought them the most joy.

God has already made us all complete. The joys we seek outside ourselves are already within each of us. Striving to see what God sees and desiring to be used as His expression is what reveals our true contentment and satisfaction. The willingness to change our view of ourselves, to accept the spiritual view of things, is the answer.

Any worthy venture must originate from an infinite idea, which can only come from God. For this reason, I find it wise to seek guidance on how to carry it out from the all-knowing source. Such a premise includes just the right activities for the business to have a lasting impact, continually evolving into higher expressions of infinite ways to bless.

Whatever our work may be, if it is done with the purpose of blessing, it cannot help but bless us and others in return. The song written by Ina D. Ogdon in 1913 comes to Mind. It was one of my father's favourites, often used to teach us the discipline of doing our best in whatever task we were given. Let me share the words here—they may stir the inherent good within you to do your best:

1.

Do not wait until some deed of greatness you may do,
Do not wait to shed your light afar;
To the many duties ever near you now be true,
Brighten the corner where you are.

Refrain

Brighten the corner where you are!
Brighten the corner where you are!

Someone far from harbor, you may guide across the bar;
Brighten the corner where you are!

2.

Just above are clouded skies that you may help to clear,
Let not narrow self your way debar;
Though into one heart alone may fall your song of cheer,
Brighten the corner where you are.

3.

Here for all your talent, you may surely find a need,
Here reflect the bright and Morning Star;
Even from your humble hand, the Bread of Life may feed,
Brighten the corner where you are.

Let us see what insights we can gain from our next chapter on
SUPPLY, MONEY, AND INCOME.

CHAPTER SEVEN

SUPPLY, MONEY, AND INCOME

"Son, thou art ever with me, and all that I have is thine."

Luke 15:31

Wherever did we get the idea that we cannot do anything without money? Money has been given an unwarranted position. We have displaced the power of God with paper.

The idea of supply being spiritual was once daunting to me. Somehow, I had always thought of supply as money. But money, in and of itself, is only paper; it is the spiritual value behind it that gives it meaning. As a child of God, I already possess spiritual value. When we hold to this Truth, it naturally finds expression in our lives—whether as money to pay bills or as any other form of material provision.

Money is simply a symbol of our ability to express certain qualities: gratitude, appreciation, honesty, kindness, and respect for one another. These are the actual values behind our money—the things we ought to cherish and claim as inherent to our being. And these qualities can be equally expressed in every part of the world, regardless of colour, education, or social background.

Our sufficiency is eternal if we see it as coming constantly from God. When we believe our supply comes from a job or a particular sale, we place limits on it. The supply appears to end once the sale is over or the job is lost. But when we understand sufficiency as ability derived from an ever-present God, we identify with an ever-providing source.

We may feel insecure without a large bank account, investments, or a job that covers all the bills. But are any of these equal to absolute trust in the infinite resources through which God meets our needs? No matter how much money we amass, we should be careful not to make it our source of security. It should never be our surety, nor should it take the place of the everlasting, unchanging knowledge of God as ALL. Recent events have shown the danger of trusting in financial investments. The stock market fell, and accounts plummeted; people panicked, placing their security in something unstable. The only unchanging source is God, who will always supply our needs.

Our true supply is the wealth of health, happiness, satisfaction, right activity, sincere relationships, intelligence, and the ability to admire others' successes. These attributes are part of our very being. They are our real wealth. They are our true income, in any form that God has given them. Who can measure the wealth of strength, energy, joy, and rest?

Our supply is infinite because infinite good is its source. Sometimes supply comes in the form of ideas, gifts that cost nothing. For example, it may occur to me to pair one item of clothing with another in a new way, saving me from making an unnecessary purchase. Insights like these free us from the belief that our provision is tied to a specific job or material circumstance.

It is this kind of confidence in the infinity of God's supply that allows us to remain honest. Knowing God is forever looking out for us, we should ask Him what we need to do if an employer demands that we perform a dishonest task. We should not be fearful about leaving a job if that is what we are led to do. Taking such a stand reflects progress in our growth and trust in God as our everlasting source of supply.

When we ask God for specific things, we are outlining limited means for His provision. The Bible says in Isaiah 55:8, "neither are your ways my ways," so we should be willing to let Him determine how our needs will be met. We simply cannot do anything better than what God's infinite Spirit can do.

Once, at the airport, I overheard two men talking about their investments. One of them was confidently telling the other about what his father was going to leave him. These things are not necessarily bad, but we must be cautious not to depend on them as the source of our security. I wondered—did that man also possess heavenly riches? Our needs are many, and money alone could never satisfy them all. We cannot buy the most important things in life. And we cannot fully trust God alone as our source of unending supply if we are still depending on investments or large bank accounts. I did not truly realise this until I reached a point where I had nothing left to rely on. Then I saw that I never have to limit my source of supply to income from work, the outcome of a service provided, or a sale I made. The supply of a child of God is unlimited, and it can come from inexhaustible avenues.

A woman once told me she was upset because her daughter had decided to attend hairdressing school after high school. I asked her whether her daughter seemed to Love that idea and whether she had a natural gift for hairdressing. The mother said, "Oh yes, she can do anybody's hair." I reassured her that if this was what God had planned for her daughter, then she would shine in that line of work, because she would not be doing it merely as a source of income.

During our conversation, it emerged that she and her husband had hoped their daughter would become a doctor or a lawyer. They felt she was intelligent enough to pursue something with more income potential and greater prestige. She added that her daughter felt so strongly about her choice that she was prepared to leave home if her decision became a source of conflict. However, after we spoke, the mother seemed more at peace.

That daughter could have had enough to meet all her needs if she followed what she loved and was naturally gifted in. There is no reason we should not have truly intelligent hairdressers; all people are, after all, the expression of the same Mind. Choosing a career out of rebellion against her parents would have been wrong, but I was confident God would guide her to the right decision. I never heard from her again, but I trust that if they relied on God, the right outcome followed.

We entrone money when we allow it to dictate what schools we want our children to attend or what professions we expect them to follow. This experience caused me to look deeply into myself and ask whether I had been wilfully directing my own children's paths. I do not mean to say we should never guide them, but we must always trust the guidance of the ultimate Parent and never lose sight of the Truth that He has a right place for everyone.

"My grace is sufficient" (2 Corinthians 12:9). How can we say all is well if we have no money to pay our bills? It is because money is only a part of our supply. If we focused more on the Truth of the sufficiency of God's grace, rather than dwelling so much on how we can make money, we would not overlook the many ideas always ready for implementation to meet our needs.

We all know that fires and floods can cause all material to vanish in just seconds. Does it not make sense, then, to make God, who can never be touched, the source that can always provide?

The story of the prodigal son, found in Luke 15:11-32, holds deep meaning for me now. I used to look at it quite literally, but there is also a spiritual interpretation. The story represents how we have left our Father's home of spiritual peace to dwell in the frivolity of materialism. It is reassuring to know that when we awaken to the true value of Life in God, we can repent and return to our Father's house, where we are received into His loving arms.

Like the prodigal, I woke up to the Truth that I cannot lack when my Father has all things. I must see myself as one who has never truly lacked. I am a beloved child of God, complete with all that my Father has. That includes money and every other good thing He has prepared for me. The only thing I ever lacked—and many still lack—is the right understanding of God and the knowledge of my true selfhood.

When the prodigal son returned, his loving father embraced him and welcomed him with great joy. I, too, can return to my Father in thought, affirm His Love for me, and begin to benefit from right thinking. The father said to the son who had remained at home, "Son, thou art ever with me and all that I have is thine." (Luke 15:31). This means that as long as I am at home with my Father, all good is mine to enjoy and be grateful for.

We pay a heavy price when we enthrone money and make it the cause rather than the effect. Its shackles are weighty and can imprison for a long time. The focus on money often seems to halt our ideas in their tracks. We say, "If I had the money, I would do this or that," and when we do not see the money, we feel that we cannot do what we are meant to do.

We must reconsider the role of money and ensure it remains in its rightful place in our thinking. It is not only the wealthy who are able to do good or bring about change in the world. Whether we have much or little, our availability to be used for a good purpose, as God has planned, supersedes our bank accounts and any other material possessions.

What gains the reward is not simply the work itself, but the spiritual qualities expressed through our actions: faithfulness, truthfulness, dignity, respect, orderliness, punctuality, and loyalty. In Ruth 2, it was Ruth's loyalty that led her to stay with Naomi and to glean corn alongside Boaz's men. This loyalty was rewarded when Boaz married her and provided for her needs. Ruth not only gained material wealth but was also blessed with a loving husband and a child. No amount of physical work, even with good wages, could have fulfilled her needs to that extent.

After many years of work in our family business, there came a time when I felt utterly unable to continue. I felt pulled in many directions. But because of the Truths I had been learning about God, I surrendered to be used according to His will. That sincere desire opened the way for my experience in healing ministry. I believe that willingness was rewarded beyond anything I could have planned for myself. That is why Jesus said, "Seek ye first the kingdom of God and his righteousness; and all these shall be given unto you . . ." (Matthew 6:33).

Discover your true nature and live the qualities that are yours as a child of God, and all else will be given to you.

In Proverbs 8:18-21, we read, "Riches and honour are with me; yea, durable riches and righteousness. My fruit is better than gold, yea, than fine gold; and my revenue than choice silver. I lead in the way of righteousness, in the midst of the paths of judgment: That I may cause those that love me to inherit substance; and I will fill their treasures."

There is a serious wrong being done in the name of good that must be corrected. If we attempt to solve the world's problems materially, we will never find lasting solutions to the falsities that plague us. Many philanthropic measures and humanitarian efforts in Africa—such as the distribution of rice and wheat—achieve only short-term goals. Good is not withheld because people lack access to it; the lack itself stems from a false belief in lack. The same God who provided food in the wilderness is infinitely good and can never cease to provide.

I am a princess, and I know it—so why should I live like a pauper? A pauper's thinking keeps him there. He believes she cannot do better because he only trusts what he sees, and he sees so little. What he truly needs is an awakening to his real identity as the spiritual image and likeness of God. He must be reminded that the Father's goodness is for all His children. His humble persistence in this Truth can free him from fear and lead him to the realisation of the abundance already present for him.

This transformation demands some discipline of thought, which is possible for everyone. I had to constantly lift my gaze to the everlasting source and expect that the supply would manifest in God's own way. No longer did I look to my income from work as my sole provision. Thus, when I went to interviews, I never thought *I must have this job because my supply depends on it.* I simply expected good, and I trusted that I would receive the good that God had prepared. In Psalm 34:10, we read, "... they that seek the Lord shall not want any good thing."

I have asked myself many times whether a loving, impartial, and good God would bless only a particular race with all his goodness, while others of His own creation continually suffer lack. Yet God is everywhere, and His ideas are infinite, so everyone has equal access to these divine ideas. People either do not know this blessing, or they allow false education to block them from seeing the truth.

Even in the poorest village, one can usually find at least one wealthy person who is also good and happy. I am not speaking about the kind of rich man imprisoned by his riches. I am sure you, too, know people who are wealthy yet so mean-spirited and unhappy that many so-called "poor" people would prefer to remain without wealth if that is what being rich looks like.

People need to understand that they are not victims of circumstance, and they should be encouraged to feel God's Love and presence right where they are. We must all take to heart what is written in the Bible: "And his allowance was a continual allowance given him of the king, a daily rate for every day, all the days of his life" (2 Kings 25:30). We are assured again by, "Son, ...thou art ever with me and all that I have is thine" (Luke 15:31).

"Divine love always has met and always will meet every human need" (*Science and Health with Key to the Scriptures*, Eddy, page 494). Jesus demonstrated this conviction so clearly in how He was never disturbed by apparent discord. To Him, only the presence of God's goodness was real. He perceived this perfection wherever He was, even when confronted with sickness, lack, or death.

If I know I already possess something, I do not go searching for it frantically. I listen quietly for direction. The practical steps unfold, and what is mine is revealed to me. I am sure we have all experienced those times when we needed something, and then it appeared in the most mysterious and timely way.

I like the thought that no bank account assures my security, and neither does the loss of one affect my real security. This captures the need to view income and supply from a spiritual perspective. When I first encountered this idea, I wondered how it could be practical. Then I came to understand that if I needed money to pay a bill, I could rely on the qualities of Life, Truth, and Love to supply the need. My income from Truth would be expressed in purity, gratitude, selflessness, and the wholesomeness that includes right activity. If I see myself in terms of these spiritual qualities, then the question becomes: *how can someone who is so fulfilled lack anything?*

Think of the lengths to which some people will go to gain money. Since money remains the modern medium of exchange, it is reasonable that we need to use it. But it is the misunderstanding of its power—the exaggerated belief in its control—that is so damaging. We live, and therefore, we use money. We do not have to have money in order to live. If this Truth were more widely understood, we would be less often tempted by the fear of not having enough. That fear has led many "good" people to abandon honourable work for something dishonourable, believing it will solve their financial problems, even if it compromises their integrity.

As Proverbs 28:8, 20: "He that by usury and unjust gain increaseth his substance, he shall gather it for him that will pity the poor. A faithful man shall abound with blessings, but he that maketh haste to be rich shall not be innocent."

And from Ecclesiastes 5:10-12: "He that loveth silver shall not be satisfied with silver; nor he that loveth abundance with increase: this is also vanity. When goods increase, they are increased that eat them: and what good is there to the owners thereof, saving the beholding of them with their eyes? The sleep of a labouring man is sweet, whether he eat little or much: but the abundance of the rich will not suffer him to sleep."

1 Timothy 6:10, 17-19: "For the love of money is the root of all evil: which, while some coveted after, they have erred from the faith and pierced themselves through with many sorrows. Charge them that are rich in this world, that they be not high-minded, nor trust in uncertain riches, but in the living God, who giveth us richly all things to enjoy; That they do good, that they be rich in good works, ready to distribute, willing to communicate; Laying up in store for themselves a good foundation . . . that leads to eternal life."

Job 31:24, 28: "If I have made gold my hope, or have said to the fine gold, Thou art my confidence; This also were an iniquity to be punished by the judge: for I should have denied the God that is above."

Let us gain the correct view of money and relegate it to its rightful place in our life experience. This is the only way to stop it from dominating us. God must be first in all we do, for every good thing comes from Him. Money is a tool to be used for good, but it is the good that brings the joy and satisfaction, not the money itself.

Let us see what insights we can gain from our next chapter on **HEALTH OR SICKNESS**.

CHAPTER EIGHT

HEALTH OR SICKNESS

"Heal the sick, cleanse the lepers, raise the dead, cast out devils: freely ye have received, freely give."

Matt 10:8

It is clear that we must understand God and trust in Him more than we trust in our belief in sickness. Jesus readily bestowed blessings when He discerned great faith in someone. This is evident throughout His healing ministry: when people showed faith in God's power to heal, they were healed. We see this in the case of the centurion (Matthew 8:5-10), the man whose friends put him through the roof (Mark 2:3-5), and the woman with the issue of blood (Matthew 9:19-22).

Jesus often acknowledged the faith of those He healed, saying, "... thy faith hath made thee whole" (Matthew 9:22). Those who came, yearning for healing, must have trusted the divine power Jesus expressed. This emphasis on faith in God invites us to examine ourselves: do we believe more in the power of sickness, or in the power of God and the promise of good health?

We all know that health is the opposite of sickness. While health denotes our wholeness, sickness refers to a disruption of that wholeness. Health also implies soundness of Mind. Mrs. Eddy writes in *Science and Health with Key to the Scriptures*, "A sick body is evolved from sick thoughts" (SH pg. 260: 20-21).

Do you not sometimes wonder how many people might enjoy better health if we were not constantly bombarded by talk of symptoms, treatments, and the long list of things we are told to avoid in order to stay well? Do you not question how much money might be saved if sickness occupied less space in our conversations?

Even our social conversations are often dominated by talk of which doctor someone is seeing and why, the latest health trends, or the medications being taken. This constant focus on disease reflects just how deeply we believe in the reality and the power of illness.

Yet in Exodus 23:25, we read, "And ye shall serve the Lord your God, and he shall bless thy bread, and thy water; and I will take sickness away from the midst of thee." If sickness were something God intended us to have, He would not remove it. And if sickness were a legitimate or necessary part of our existence, why did Jesus devote so much of His ministry to healing the sick and the sinful?

Jesus also said, "... He that believeth on me, the works that I do shall he do also; and greater works than these shall he do;" (John 14:12). We are not required to tolerate sickness. We could vanquish it if only we trusted the Truth about ourselves.

When I worked in a chronic pain clinic, I encountered patients who left their jobs, turned to alcohol, and abused drugs in an effort to convince themselves and others that their pain was real—and that nothing could bring them relief. One of the most extreme cases we saw was a woman who took fifty pills a day.

Our well-being is embodied in consciousness, so a purer consciousness of oneself maybe one of the most effective forms of preventive health—one that each of us can engage in without any cost to our national budget. Health is associated with soundness of Mind, purity, and goodness. Clearly, we cannot continue to ignore the effect of this constant focus on all that can go wrong while still seeking lasting solutions to our health concerns.

Heal the sick. This sounds imperative. It reads as a command to rid ourselves of this falsity called sickness. When Jesus healed the man with palsy, He said, " . . . .Son, be of good cheer; thy sins be forgiven thee." (Matthew 9:2). And later, He warned against returning to sin in John 5:14: " . . . .Behold, thou art made whole: sin no more, lest a worse thing come unto thee." He must have considered it sinful to believe in the reality of sickness, for accepting sickness would be a denial of God's perfection—and of our own, as His reflection.

I once worked as a health visitor in England, where the role was focused primarily on preventive health. I found that much of our attention was directed toward the body, what to eat, proper hygiene, and recommended exercises. Yet there was a noticeable lack of attention to the state of thought. And thought, after all, has a profound effect on our sense of wholeness.

In midwifery, too, much of our contribution to childbirth was centred on how to minimise pain and prevent complications. Yet this approach assumed that childbirth must be painful. There was little acknowledgment of the almightiness of the divine involvement in something as sacred and beautiful as childbirth. Our individual right-thinking could contribute to a collective atmosphere of greater peace and strength during such an experience.

We should obey the command to heal the sick, even if we are not healing others ourselves. It is clear that even Jesus recognised it was not Him, the man Jesus, who healed. He said, "My Father worketh hitherto, and I work." (John 5:17).

If we followed the Truths that allow the healing Spirit of God to be reflected in us, we too could heal.

When it dawned on me that I had entertained a false sense of self as material rather than spiritual, all the beliefs associated with that wrong premise became obvious. I started to feel uncomfortable at work, even though one might say, as a registered nurse, I was helping people.

My thoughts were changing, in direct opposition to my career in medical nursing. Granted, I had compassion for my patients and genuinely wanted them to get better. I was cheerful, gentle, and tender. But I needed to resolve the premise from which I viewed my patients. As a medical nurse, I accepted as *real* the very illnesses from which they needed healing.

I accepted every patient as Mr. or Mrs. A in the hospital with diabetes, chronic bronchitis, emphysema, or whatever the diagnosis was. When I saw Mrs. A, I thought of diabetes, and diabetes became her identity. Even my sympathy for her reinforced the reality of the disease. Like many nurses, I would research the possible complications of diabetes and study them so I could immediately recognise symptoms and report them or carry out the appropriate medical procedures.

At the same time, the specific drugs I administered as healing agents had the expected effect. The patient might go home with a temporary or unchanged belief about herself. The latent fears she held about her illness remained, only to manifest at some later date. Sometimes, patients are left with an even stronger conviction of what their diagnoses are, expecting to live with them for the rest of their lives.

Often, a recommended lifestyle change intended to keep an illness subdued would further enslave an already frightened patient. What long-term benefit could there be for someone who leaves the hospital feeling better in body, but still holds the same sick identity in thought, along with all the fears connected to the diagnosis?

At home, her conversation might include phrases such as *my diabetes*. If I were to see Mrs. A now, I might ask, "Who gave it to you, and who said you have to own it forever?"

If we never allow someone to call us a thief, why do we so readily accept what others label us with when it is an illness? This stands in direct contradiction to what God has said about us.

I also noticed during my medical nursing practice that we tend to try everything else before turning wholeheartedly to God for help. We have all heard people say, "We've done everything we can do; it's up to God now." The order of our actions is startling. Even when we say we turn to God first, our faith is often still in what the doctor will say or what prescription will be given. We may simply have more faith in that material reality than in the certainty that God never created diseases, or in His power to heal. Our radical reliance on God is tested when sickness appears.

Many argue that God gave doctors the intelligence to heal through drugs. This was one point that took some resolving. I understood such thinking is reasonable as long as we are thinking from a material perspective. But when I understood and wholeheartedly accepted the

Truth that all is good, I began to see why even those things that appear good (such as medicines) must ultimately yield to the spiritual view, if we desire to realise our true freedom.

Our usual instinct to flee from danger seems completely forgotten when it comes to sickness. We should protest this sickness that appears, just as we would protest anything else that offends or violates our sense of rightness. Jesus's handling of discord makes this clear. He showed us how to respond when faced with the illusion of sickness.

"Verily, verily, I say unto you, He that believeth on me, the works that I do shall he do also; and greater works than these shall he do" (John 14:12). Truth was His panacea for every discord. Why do we not use the Truth as our most potent antidote to the illusion of sickness?

I remember the fear I witnessed in patients even after successful surgeries. Going home with instructions about lifestyle changes often left them holding on to an image of themselves as still attached to the illness. Once, I cared for a judge who had undergone heart surgery. The procedure had gone well, and he was discharged. But what I found, as his nurse at home, was a fearful, middle-aged man, deeply anxious about his future. This fear persisted because the illness had become part of his identity. He now saw himself as a heart patient, his Life marked by new restrictions that constantly reminded him of what he had endured.

When Jesus healed, the people returned to their original, perfect state—what God had created. When He healed Simon's wife's mother, she immediately ministered to them (Mark 1:31). Jesus saw only the perfection that God had created, even when confronted with sickness. He saw the purity and the perfection of God's children. Jesus never attended any school to study anatomy, physiology, pharmacology, or disease processes. He healed by knowing what was true about God's creation.

Years ago, the pastor of the church I attended shared a testimony about a healing he had received through prayer. He said he had tried many material cures to no avail. One night, frightened and feeling as though he was taking his last breath, he cried out to God, "Save me!" At that moment, he felt a deep sense of calm, and all fear left him. From then on, he was led to read various Bible texts, which helped to restore his sense of good health.

What struck me as interesting while listening to this was the order in which he, a pastor, had gone about handling his illness. He had tried everything else first. That was honest, because even though he had been praying, his faith had been in the medications and in the doctor's advice. Like him, we often say we will try what medical science can do first, and if that does not help, we will try God. Something is wrong with this order.

In the hospital, I encountered many situations like this—where unfamiliarity with the Bible, or disbelief in an unseen power, was evident. Often, people resorted to a last-minute cry to God. Their thoughts were so entrenched in the material picture that it was difficult for them even to find interest in reading the Bible. They may have had it at their bedside, but there was no reading going on, and certainly no faith in what it had to say.

Those who placed their reliance on God seemed less frightened, no matter the presenting circumstances. They often had a loving familiarity with Bible verses and hymns. Their thoughts were calm because faith in the unseen power helped them become aware of the ever-present Love that surrounds all of us, whether we are conscious of it or not.

The pastor gave his full reliance to God only on the night he cried out for help; his readiness to let the light in banished his fear. We should seek God first, in all sincerity, faith, and humility, and allow Him to direct even the human steps we are to take when faced with any form of illness.

While we put off our deliverance from sin, fooling ourselves into thinking we are happy in our wrongdoing, most people overtly wish for immediate relief from the pain of sickness. But to forsake sin always brings better health. After Jesus healed the cripple at the pool of Bethesda, He later said to him in the temple; "Behold, thou art made whole: sin no more, lest a worse thing come unto thee." (John 5:14). It is often anger, fear, resentment, hate, envy, sinful indulgence in certain appetites, and jealousy which are the real diseases. The symptoms are simply manifestations of wrong beliefs and thoughts we have accepted as our own.

How can a group of *so-called* alcoholics, who share the false belief that they are indeed alcoholics, help one another? The same is true of focus groups for obesity or any other mistaken identity. In such groups, the premise of false identity dooms the expected outcome for many. Hence, we hear statements like, "I have not taken a drink in two years, but I know I'll always be an alcoholic." Who said so? Such thinking cannot be helpful to anyone.

We should be engaged in thoughts that help us see ourselves as God, our Creator, sees us. We cannot experience permanent healing in any other way. There should be a group of breast cancer survivors who say, "It was never true in God's view," not "yes, it is true, and it could happen to someone else."

I once observed a woman, very ill in her bed, look with resentment and disdain at her brother. He had come to visit her upon learning of her illness, and all she could do, even then, was express hatred. She seemed to be suffering from the hate as much as from the illness. She asked that her brother not be allowed to remain in her room. If one continues to believe in one's sickness while also holding on to resentment, is it possible to allow the light of God to lead the way out of illness? Love cannot dwell where hate or resentment exists. She may have been feeling her brother's resentment toward her, but she could not help herself by resenting him in return. The only real power is in loving—the kind of loving that sees one's true selfhood.

So much in our lives is hinged on the belief in illness, to the extent that people bypass the work God has for them to do, simply because health insurance is their first concern when accepting a job. We do not ask if this is what God wants us to do; instead, we are more concerned with whether the position includes health insurance, as if getting sick is guaranteed.

In a Pain Unit where I worked, there were people who had been described as having intractable (continuous) pain. Yet most of them could go hours without any complaints when they were happily engaged in activities that took their thoughts off the illusion of pain.

I am confident that God's perfect work was finished, and this fact cannot be changed. This vision sustains the hope that, sooner or later, our perfection will be realised. Should we not, like Jesus, ask the sick whether they truly want to be healed, and what they are willing to let go of in order to be healed? Jesus treated moral wrongdoing as seriously as physical illness. To the adulterous woman, Jesus said, "Neither do I condemn thee: go, *and sin no more*." (John 8:11).

We certainly go too far when we begin claiming certain illnesses are associated with certain skin colours. God created all races perfectly. Those who are perpetually labelled as poor are often the same people seen as the primary sufferers of a disease. But what kind of God would favour only some of His children? We do not have to accept this. God loves ALL His children.

The Bible speaks of an impartial God in Acts 10:34-35. "... .God is no respecter of persons: But in every nation he that feareth him, and worketh righteousness, is accepted with him." He could not give some of His own creation certain illnesses and make others healthy. However, we hesitate to accept our completeness. The idea of our real selves being perfect is sometimes too much to grasp. But God is saying this to us.

All of this has been proven in my own experience. When our oldest daughter was born, she was healthy. Then, after a couple of doctor visits, we were told that she had sickle cell anaemia—a blood abnormality often associated with Black people. On one of our visits, the doctor said that our daughter would have to take penicillin for the rest of her life. Even then, before I had gained the spiritual understanding I now have, I sensed there was something troubling about such a statement.

I must admit, although my husband and I refused that treatment, we still carried with us part of what had become our daughter's identity. This belief led to certain precautions we took to prevent her from getting infections. Each time she seemed sick, we feared what might follow based on the diagnosis. As I grew in the understanding of man's perfection, I became more able to fearlessly deny any symptoms that appeared to be a part of her.

What finally broke the mesmerism of this lie, which had lingered in my thoughts for almost thirty years, occurred one day in New York. I had never entirely shaken the idea that she genuinely had what the doctor said she had. Every time she told me she felt unwell, my thoughts returned to the diagnosis. I prayed to know the Truth about her. A few days prior to this experience, it came to me very clearly: I needed to know her perfection.

On this day, I felt strongly that I should know the Truth. I noticed that my niece had called three times. When I returned her call, she said that my daughter was in the hospital. I am still amazed at how calm I was in that moment. I was not afraid. I stood still and simply knew, with heartfelt gratitude and conviction, that she is perfect, and I left the entire situation in the Father's hands.

When I was able to speak to her, she sounded quiet but not afraid, and she said they wanted to run some tests. I reassured her of her real identity. Within a couple of days, she was released from the hospital, and this time, nothing abnormal was said about her blood.

The belief in obesity has now become a problem of epidemic proportions. Although I have never been severely overweight, there were times in my adult life when I was heavy enough to feel uneasy. During those seasons, I tried several popular weight management methods and learned a great deal. The greatest lesson was this: losing weight without a lasting thought adjustment about oneself is never enough. I once saw someone lose one hundred pounds, only to gain it all back. He also became so depressed that he wanted to take his life. I have also met people who lose weight but still feel just as overweight as before.

Is there then a spiritual approach to effective weight loss? There is only one lasting solution to any problem—we must seek answers from a spiritual viewpoint. We must consider whether much of obesity is not a manifestation of heavy, wrong thinking. We must align our thoughts with the ideas and Truths found in the Bible if we want to gain the answers we seek. Many people have simply lost the false sense of appetite after they have diligently sought to know more about God. " . . . that he might make thee know that man doth not live by bread only, but by every word that proceedeth out of the mouth of the LORD . . . " (Deuteronomy 8:3). And Jesus's counsel, "For my yoke is easy and my burden is light" (Matthew 11:30).

When I dropped false thoughts, I lost weight effortlessly. I felt less hungry and thought less about food. Instead of eating to comfort myself in response to some uncomfortable thoughts, I felt comforted by spiritual ideas. There is no need for the word of God to be satisfied if wholeheartedly applied. My desire to overeat was really a false sense, and I had the power not to respond to it. The key was to persist in *unknowing* all the wrong thoughts I had been carrying.

Unless we change our thought models, much of what we do is in vain. This change does not come through human will or positive thinking, but through the humble and grateful knowing that God is All and is only good. In this way, we can replace a false sense of obesity with the true understanding of ourselves as God's children, who have always been perfect.

I am not condemning the material measures that are in use, but recognising that there is a permanent solution—one that comes only through understanding God and man as part of His perfect creation—that leads to a reformation of consciousness that brings lasting and greater peace.

The belief in old age and its woes should be substituted with the idea that growing older means growing in spiritual wisdom and Truth, not deterioration of the body or faculties. The Bible gives us many instances where what seemed impossible was accomplished by people considered to be old.

Medical complications and the beliefs surrounding them continue to enslave us, even if temporary relief has been achieved. It is therefore important not to stray from the Truth that God alone is the Creator. He never created disease, and it is our birthright to overcome it.

When faced with the evil of a severe illness, why do we simply accept that we will die? Why do we not turn immediately to Life (God) and feel His Love for us? Turning to God would give us more strength to confront the illness, rather than allowing it to take over our dominion. But something is required of us. We turn to God and feel His Love *if* we have been living the Truth, as in: "If ye abide in me, and my words abide in you, ye shall ask what ye will, and it shall be done unto you" (John 15:7, 8).

I learned something that brought me great comfort when my mother passed on. In the beginning, it was difficult to free my thoughts from the finality that often seems to accompany death. The idea of eternal Life was hard to grasp.

As I began to think more deeply about the Truth that the essence of our Life is spiritual, the idea that the body is not our Life became quite clear for the first time when a friend passed on.

I was called to this friend's apartment one morning, shortly after opening our store. It was a great shock—he had visited us the previous evening and showed no signs of distress. On the way there, I could think of nothing to ease my sorrow but the new insight that Life is eternal. Prior to leaving the store, I also called a Christian Science practitioner to support my prayer—to help me hold to the Truth about Life. She affirmed the Truth of my friend's continued Life as the spiritual image and likeness of God.

When I arrived, his roommate and another man were present, waiting for the police to arrive. My friend lay on his bed, fully dressed.

There was no visible change in his appearance. Somehow, the fact that Life is spiritual came to me very clearly. I thought, if the body is still here, unchanged, and yet he is no longer moving, then something else must animate man—and that something cannot be contained in the body. The thought was so clear, it was as if someone were telling me that his real Life could not be touched by anything. And that is what continues: the immortal, spiritual self.

I have used this insight to comfort myself often whenever someone mentions the death of another. Then, when my mother passed on, I was to read in church that Sunday. At first, I accepted the circumstances that I understood had led to her death. But then I realised I had to hold on to the Truth in order to be able to read. So, once again, with the help of a Christian Science practitioner, I turned to the Truth of Life eternal.

I held firmly to the fact that nothing that had taken place could have touched the perfect, spiritual identity of my mother. I felt an enveloping sense of Love all around me, and with that, I was able to read better than I ever had before. I thought I could continue to love her, just as she continues to love me. Her smile became very vivid to me, which was a great comfort.

From that point on, my grief was considerably lessened. Each time the thought of never seeing her again came to Mind, I felt reassured that I could still love her and know that she loves me as well. Nothing else could have given me such comfort, and I cherish that experience. I am grateful for it and share it so that others may also experience the peace offered by the promise of eternal Life.

I am so grateful that, over the years, my conviction in Life eternal has comforted me and helped me quickly find peace when others have passed on. It has also enabled me to comfort others in my work as a

Christian Science Practitioner. Could this be what is meant by, "Oh death, where is thy sting?" (1 Corinthians 15:55).

Let us see what insights we can gain from our next chapter on **GRATITUDE, HAPPINESS, AND JOY.**

CHAPTER NINE

GRATITUDE, HAPPINESS, AND JOY

"Giving Thanks Always For All Things unto God and the Father . . . "

Ephesians 5: 20

" . . . Alleluia: for the Lord God omnipotent reigneth.
Let us be glad and rejoice, and give honour to him:"

Revelation 19:6, 7

Often, I open my eyes and say, "Thank God" for Life, because I know He is Life itself. I wake up to the unchanging Truth that we are held in the everlasting arms of God, protecting, blessing, and loving us. This alone is enough to be thankful for all day. There was a time when I was so blinded by fear, worry, and anxiety that I could not even think of the infinite blessings I should be thankful for.

Our gratitude for all the good things we receive should be expressed with humble and genuine thanksgiving to God. We must never forget that every good thing, however small, comes from God; every movement has its origin in God.

If someone gives us something and we are truly grateful for it, we cherish it. We may frequently wear it, use it, or look at it. The frequency of our contact with that item shows that our words of gratitude are backed by an activity that demonstrates gratitude. We love being with that item. Similarly, nothing should stop us from showing our gratitude for God's grace by constantly practicing His demands. Only the lives we choose to live can demonstrate our genuine gratitude for His blessings.

If we are grateful for how we have been blessed, we should be using the Truth Jesus taught to improve our lives and the lives of others. Each day, we apply the spiritual truths found in the Bible to demonstrate the goodness that God created. Gratitude should not be expressed in words alone—my gratitude empowers me in my daily life.

When fear tempts me, I remember that Love is always greater than hate or resentment, that justice is superior to injustice, and that my purity as a child of God is more powerful than any imperfection that claims to define me. Gratitude is my expression of loyalty to the Truth.

It is my constant prayer to learn more about God, to hear His voice, and to obey it. This keeps my thoughts centred on God and brings a calm I did not always have. That calm is not the result of self-discipline, but the fruit of cultivating an awareness that compares my experiences with the knowledge that God is always supreme. He is the ultimate governing power; therefore, there is no need to fear. This is the reward for placing faith in God and trusting Him, as illustrated in Hebrews 11:6.

Gratitude should be expressed as a demonstration of the super-abundance that awaits mankind. No one is in lack, because abundance is for everyone. Hoarding cannot make anyone richer in what is truly valuable and unseen because it is limitless, and all have equal access to it. God loves us all too much for us to believe that riches come only through hard work. To tie availability to education, or to any finite qualification, is to place a limit on God.

The only genuine way to give is to demonstrate superabundance, the superabundance that belongs to all. Any giving that says, "*here you are because you lack,*" is giving without Love. Such giving views the recipient as limited, whereas God assures us that good awaits all. If I am giving to Africans, and I believe I am doing so because they do not have, then I am thinking wrongly about a people who are also created by God. True giving must be the evidence of the receiver's abundance, as well as the giver's.

To be able to give with joy reinforces one's own sense of abundance. I remember when I used to tithe more out of duty, or simply because I believed it was something I was supposed to do, rather than from a place of cheerful giving, grounded in the understanding of my own rich overflow. I now understand that it is my corrected sense of having, rooted in the knowledge that my source is infinite, that supplies my every need, not the act of tithing itself. To give freely is a joyful act.

When your thoughts are focused on the omnipotence of God, your realisation of freedom becomes so clear that it manifests. Loving others and seeing them rightly makes giving more joyous. Through giving, you disprove the claim that anyone could be outside the infinite circle of an all-providing Love. Part of unceasing prayer must be the continual embrace of all humanity in this great Love.

Where I see pride, I am grateful to know humility is the unchanging reality. Where there is selfishness, I insist on the unseen selflessness. Where there is injustice, I know that justice is of God and is ever-present. There is deep gratitude in knowing that Truth will always be superior to evil, innocence will always conquer guilt, humility will always supersede pride, Love will always triumph over hate, courage will always defeat fear, honesty will always vanquish shame, and justice will ultimately overthrow injustice. God is everywhere present; therefore, Good is always at hand.

Much has been written about gratitude and how it helps to heal the heart. Gratitude calms my thoughts and leads me to answers I might otherwise miss. I have literally taken pen and paper to write down what I am grateful for. It is amazing how much I can take for granted if I do not make the effort to thank God each morning and at night for all the good that appears throughout the day.

One day, I was thinking about the images of poverty, hunger, and disease in Africa, and how often the continent is almost identified with woe. Yet it is hypocritical to say that God is everywhere, while continuing to believe there are places in the world beyond the reach of God's provision.

In the wilderness, the people did not need to do much to eat. Food was provided. "And the children of Israel did eat manna forty years, until they came to a land inhabited;" (Exodus 16:35). So, who says the same cannot happen today? Did God only perform a one-time miracle? Surely the same all-knowing source must have the lasting answers to the problems of hunger and poverty. We Love best when we are willing to change our view of people everywhere—when we look beyond what the eyes tell us and humbly seek Divine guidance to reveal the abundance that is always present.

Africa dwells within this same God. Human efforts to bring food and clothing to parts of Africa are meaningful, but material-based relief alone does not always awaken people to look within themselves for lasting answers. Even in places often described as poverty-stricken or afflicted by disease, there is still reason for gratitude. People can thank God for the land—for its vegetation, animals, birds, flowers, and one other. Though suffering seems real, gratitude for the good need not be eclipsed by sorrow. A grateful heart opens new channels for inspired, practical steps that may not have seemed possible before.

In my own experience, I often missed the simple Truth that even a little bit of gratitude for the good that is mine, as a child of God, could be the tiny light that represents His Omnipotence, Omnipresence, and Omniscience. Like a single candle shining in the darkest corner, that light began to pierce my gloomy thoughts. I needed that light because God's guidance, protecting Love, and Divine government once felt so far from me.

It must have been my sincere desire to know the Truth and a willingness to be guided that woke me up one day. I began listing all the things I could be grateful for: I was well, at least physically; all my family members were well; we lived in a safe and beautiful neighbourhood; I could go for walks and admire the many trees and flowers around me. I could be grateful that I could eat, walk, smile, think, see, hear, and sing.

So why did I not even want to hear the words *grateful, give thanks, rejoice*? It was because, in that deep-seated misery, I could not see, feel, or believe the Truth about a loving Father-Mother God, whose Love is constantly present. I was being blinded by the very thoughts I most needed to release.

I hope that if anyone reading this is going through a difficult time, they would take to heart the practice of insisting on God's ever-present power and Love. The reason for this constant expression of gratitude, regardless of what we may be experiencing, is that it helps us acknowledge the Truth of a perfect God, who has created a perfect man and a perfect universe. Whether we see it in the moment or not does not change the fact that perfection is the spiritual reality.

When you begin to be grateful for God's perfect work—which includes you—your thinking moves in the right direction, where you can begin to recognise the good around you. Continued exaltation of thought, which comes by persistently holding on to the Truth of God's perfect man, brings more light and gradually dismisses the darkness of wrong thoughts. Be sincerely grateful for everything, because that is how you kindle the tiny flame you need to guide you out of the seeming darkness.

Let us see what insights we can gain from our final chapter on **PRAYER, SAFETY, PEACE, AND TRUE FREEDOM.**

CHAPTER TEN

PRAYER, SAFETY, PEACE, AND TRUE FREEDOM

"Pray without ceasing."

1 Thessalonians 5:17

"Thou wilt keep him in perfect peace whose mind is stayed on thee."

Isaiah 26:3

"In returning and rest shall ye be saved, in quietness and in confidence shall be your strength:"

Isaiah 30:15

"He that dwelleth in the secret place of the most high shall abide under the shadow of the Almighty."

Psalm 91:1

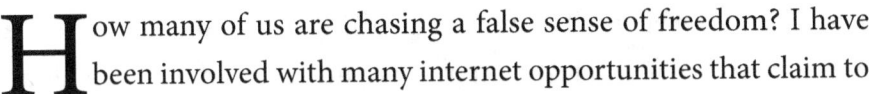

How many of us are chasing a false sense of freedom? I have been involved with many internet opportunities that claim to offer financial freedom. Unfortunately, many of them suggest that the accumulation of wealth is the actual demonstration of freedom. Not so. Clearly, they have not taken into consideration the many financially wealthy individuals who struggle with addiction, depression, unstable lifestyles, or are in a continuous search for lasting fulfilment.

The real and permanent sense of freedom is found in the acknowledgment and acceptance of the infinite source of all good. This stems from the understanding and deep conviction that we are all the children of God. This recognition brings right thinking, right knowing, and right doing. Our liberty is proved when we abide with God—when we feel His Love so near that we begin to see our real selves, what God sees as the only reality.

Like the prodigal son, I have made the commitment to return to my Father's house, where there are many mansions and enough for everyone. There, I am received with Love, and I choose to remain— to stay and receive the blessings my loving Father-Mother bestows.

Let us return to our heavenly home, and let us awaken with gratitude to all the good that has always been ours. This return is our saving grace and the foundation of our true freedom.

The psalmist said, "I will lift up mine eyes unto the hills from whence cometh my help" (Psalm 121:1). When I made the decision to diligently seek God, I became ready for a complete thought overhaul. I was willing to let God express, in me, the fullness of my true nature. This humble willingness to submit came from the difficult experiences I had while relying on human planning. I had learned my lesson, and I was ready to follow a different path.

To be materially comfortable can, at times, fool us into believing that all is well. Yet we all know that anything material can vanish in a moment. It can be exhausting to rely on human willpower to acquire and maintain what we have. There is no real freedom if we are lying awake at night, worrying about where our investments are or what our financial manager is doing with our assets.

When my husband and I owned a tropical store, we installed surveillance cameras to deter thieves. Unfortunately, the two times the store was broken into, the footage of the robbers was too blurry for identification. Later, another salesman offered to install a camera that we could monitor from home. By that point, I had begun to commit more fully to my spiritual studies. My response to him was, "If I need to watch my business twenty-four hours a day, then it is clearly too burdensome for us to continue." Where is the freedom in that? No amount of equipment or human effort can guarantee foolproof security. And yet, our clear understanding of Life in God reveals that we are constantly in His presence. We have true and lasting security from our loving Father-Mother God.

An experience from long ago clearly illustrates the supremacy of God's constant care. I had to be at the airport by 7:30 the next morning, but throughout the night I felt restless and uneasy. As morning approached, I kept hearing a quiet but persistent message urging me to go to our store. I did not want to go—it felt inconvenient, and I worried it might delay me getting to the airport on time. After several strong inner promptings, I finally prayed, asking God to guide me—to make me go if I truly needed to. On the way, I continued praying, affirming that God is everywhere, and trusting that there would be no unnecessary delays.

As I arrived and began to unlock the door of the store, I heard loud noises inside. Strangely, I remained calm. I entered and followed the sound, only to find an older, bearded man attempting to break a window in order to escape with a record player. I ran outside to call the police. He followed me briefly, then turned back. In the end, he managed to climb onto one of the deep freezers and escape.

I told the police where I had seen him go, and they immediately went in that direction. They were able to apprehend him. I was asked to identify him, and I could—by his beard—even though he had managed to change clothes in that short time.

What was humbling in this experience was that, when we took inventory to check for missing items, it became clear that he had taken nothing. Even the record player he had tried to escape with was left behind. Although the cash register had been broken open, not a single cent was missing. The police were astounded. They expressed their amazement aloud, and in that moment, I quietly offered a prayer of sincere, profound gratitude—filled with a clear awareness of God's protecting care.

I was able to write my statement, and the police used it to solve similar break-ins in the area. They were even able to recover some of the items others had reported missing. I prayed that this man would learn from this arrest and come to understand that he did not need to steal to survive. I felt God's Love for him, and I prayed he would come to see who he truly is.

Television often shows just how limited material gains really are in bringing true freedom. The wealthier some people become, the more opportunity they seem to have for indulging in enslaving appetites—whether drinking, immorality, or excess. So who is truly better off—the one who appears to have everything, yet cannot sleep at night? Or the one who may lack material wealth, but rests peacefully, secure in a clear conscience of spiritual trust?

Some people are driven to an insatiable desire to acquire more, never feeling satisfied. This endless pursuit can become a kind of enslavement, where ambition overshadows reflection. I once read in *The Telegraph* (November 2002) about a billionaire who, perhaps in search of security, lived in a penthouse equipped with state-of-the-art human security and medical care. Tragically, a fire destroyed the residence and claimed his life. He was ill, so he had nurses as well. After all the "protection" he bought, a fire destroyed the living area, including him.

I wonder what such a man could have been afraid of, because fear is a figment of our imagination, caused by some of the things we engage in or believe in. A healthy consciousness is the very best protection—one that is filled with the unsearchable Truths about God. But we have no time to think about God when we are so consumed with the fantasy that no matter how much we have, we must look for more.

Since none of us, wealthy or not, can leave our conscience behind, and knowing that it determines whether we smile or cry, it is mere foolishness or ignorance that keeps us from taking the time to cultivate a healthier conscience. We should not forget the Bible promise in Isaiah 26:3, "Thou wilt keep him in perfect peace whose mind is stayed on thee: because he trusteth in thee."

Can you see through a dirty window? Instead of waking up with thoughts of the electric bill, start your day with thoughts of God. If nothing else, thank God you woke up! One morning, I awoke with these beautiful words very clearly in thought: *When we understand the spiritual reality of all creation, we will no longer be under the mist of lies—nothing spiritual suffers, lacks, or dies because in Spirit alone are we one with God, Perfection.* I am so grateful for these messages; they bring such comfort. I find that the more I clear my thinking, the more aware I become of them. I know they are available to all.

Yielding to God's plan is essential. Humble submission to His guidance relieves us of suffering when we allow the Truth to so fill our thoughts that it dominates every wrong thought and action. This Principle will always work for our good.

Nothing can withstand the power of Truth. I like the idea of cultivating spiritual poise—remaining undisturbed by anything false that tries to convince me it is real. Only God is truly going on. I do not want a false sense of serenity, one based on everything humanly appearing to be in order, because we all know that houses, the bank accounts, and even people can vanish just as quickly as they come.

You cannot think about God and be sad, self-pitying, resentful, ungrateful, revengeful, envious, self-doubting, or lonely, because when you focus on God, false beliefs and the troubling events around us begin to lose their reality in consciousness. I realised this when my husband left his job—somehow, it was no longer frightening. I was certain he was in his right place because God keeps him there. I was no longer depending so heavily on his work as our source of supply. Supply had taken on a new meaning—a spiritual meaning that was real and lasting.

We should bless instead of judging. If God only blesses, how can we, as His reflections, justify judging others? Truth vanquishes false beliefs, and Truth cannot dwell where revenge, anger, jealousy, envy, fear, resentment, or worry reside. We should Love more, rather than be enslaved by false appetites and fears. To hold these as true is sinning, because it aligns with the lie that there is a power apart from God. All false beliefs lose their reality in our consciousness once we begin to see the light of Truth.

Luke 11:28 speaks of obedience and blessing. It does not make sense to implore God as all-powerful and then emphasise the equal presence of an opposing force. If God is all-powerful, and "every good gift is from above" as stated in James 1:17, then we ought to have confidence that we are on the side that knows no opposition. This is what Jesus did. He absolutely knew nothing but the one supreme power. He said we should follow His example—He did not say we should listen to His ways and then find our own way.

In John 8:34, we see that freedom means sinlessness, which includes identifying yourself as the expression of God. Otherwise, we imply a cause other than God. We sin when we have more than one God. Whatever occupies our thoughts becomes our God—it is what we worship. If our thoughts are consumed with money or possessions, we are worshipping them and have imprisoned ourselves.

I used to do this. I would wake up worrying about a lack. All day, I worried about insufficiency, and that same thought followed me to sleep. For a period of time, I could not shake off the fear of how we would pay the mortgage on our business building. At another time, I was preoccupied with a multilevel marketing business I was involved in. Later, it was my work that consumed my thinking. Look up Isaiah 61:1, 2, and 4 for the freeing comfort found there.

The kingdom of God, with all its spiritual qualities, is truly all we need. When we say we need clothes, food, and a house, what we are really seeking is warmth, comfort, beauty, nourishment, and security. Yet we already possess these qualities in our consciousness. These are part of the Kingdom of God within us.

Since we are God's reflection, there is nowhere we can be that He is not. In solving any problem, I know that God is helping me now. Wherever I am, I know God is with me. As St. Paul wrote in Acts 17:28, "For in him we live, and move, and have our being." We prove our Love for God by seeing His allness everywhere.

Genesis 1:27 says, "God created man(and woman) in His own image." Science and Health 516:28-29 says, "God made man in His own image, to reflect Spirit."

Colossians 3:23-24 reminds us: " . . .. .whatsoever ye do, do it heartily, as to the Lord." My correct thinking should always precede my actions.

Deuteronomy 6:7 says we should make God's laws a part of us wherever we are. We are promised power when we are obedient to God.

Here is one of those angel messages that came to me one morning: "There is nothing any one of us wants more than the peace which has its source in God."

Is it not sad that people can smile with you and yet, because of your colour or accent, believe you are less intelligent than they are? It is even sadder when I believe their lies because I do not yet know better than to reject them.

When we identify too strongly with our country of origin, we limit ourselves. During the Olympics, I heard some of the athletes emphasise "I am American," which implied they were entitled to win. Such strong identification with one's nationality may sound patriotic, but it can carry with it limiting beliefs and unfair assumptions about others. Nothing should make me think I am better than anyone else. Such thinking defies what God knows about His children.

The worthiest attributes are accessible to all mankind; all are equal in God's sight. We should be grateful that we are the children of God first, no matter where we come from. It is that realisation which frees us. What good is it to be an American, Nigerian, Algerian, or British citizen if one remains mentally enslaved? Regardless of our place of origin, it is clear we all want to feel free, perhaps more than anything else.

"I AM FREE" is the unchanging spiritual fact about me and everyone else. This freedom carries benefits that are revealed to the pure in heart. The requirement, then, is to demonstrate right thinking and right doing. It is important to begin from the premise of our spiritual identity, our freedom and perfection, because none of us can experience anything that has not first crossed our Mind. Every action is preceded by thought. Look at Jesus: the example He lived was never to forget that His presence was the Father's presence. He was always loyal to Truth. He suffered to prove the supremacy of Truth and always kept in His view the man His Father had created: pure, perfect, spiritual, and upright.

He could not tolerate any falsities of His Father's image around Him, so He healed them all to prove the omnipotence, omnipresence, omni-action, and omniscience of God. We are to do the same. We cannot perceive the perfect man while holding a critical and mistaken view of one another as mortals. Through earnest study of the Scriptures and *Science and Health*, our thoughts are uplifted, and we gain spiritual vision. Only then can we begin to see as God sees; only then can we start to understand the existence of the erfect man.

We have the ability to think and act rightly; therein lies our liberty. No person can make us free. It is our thoughts and actions, aligned with our Father's laws, which demonstrate our freedom.

It is imperative that I establish each morning which direction I am going—with the absolute Allness of God, without limitation, and without yielding to the false suggestions of other powers.

If I begin with the understanding that I am God's child, yet do not practise honesty in its fullest sense, I cannot expect to experience the pure sense of safety that comes from full obedience to divine facts.

I should not allow anything to compromise my walk with God or my obedience to His laws.

Through my study, I have learned that the continual surrender of material misconceptions increases one's spirituality. My material comforts should never be more important than upholding God's laws. This does not mean I must give up my home, my friends, or donate all my possessions to a church. Such acts, if done without spiritual understanding, have no God in them. They may stem instead from self-righteousness or a mistaken material belief that sacrifice alone makes one Holy.

God's laws are already established; what He has given us cannot be taken away. I should therefore be willing to relinquish anything I merely *believe* satisfies or completes me, and instead seek that which, when truly gained, leaves nothing lacking.

To what extent am I willing to give up the things I hold dear, with the confidence that it is impossible to lose anything that God knows I need? I once saw a preacher tell his congregation, with enthusiasm, that they should walk in the Spirit. I heard another say that harmony is there to be experienced; that you do not know what you are missing by dwelling in the material sense of things. However, I did not hear either of them point out what one must do to achieve the unseen harmony.

Walking in the Spirit is practical; it is real, and it takes place in each one's consciousness. Hence, when the gas prices rose so high and we were supposed to buy small cars, I had to bring this idea of having the right transportation into the spiritual realm.

I prayed about the need, beginning by knowing first that my perfection included no lack at all, and that included the right sense of transportation, comfort, and reliability. I knew Love's fulfilling action had already met the need. I was serious about giving the Truth my all. That understanding led to an ad in the paper about a car— comfortable and reliable—being sold by a rental company. I am grateful to a Christian healer who supported me in prayer and helped me stand with the Truth of God's loving care. I applied for the car and was approved. The interest rate was high, but I did not let it scare me, as I might have in the past.

I took the car, affirming that Love has met every need. Wrong suggestions attempted to creep in through the temptation to look at the material sense of things and say I could not afford it. This time, I was confident I had brought to light the evidence of an already fulfilled need. It was mine, and I firmly knew that everything about it would be right. I found an auto insurance rebate that had been mailed to me through my Credit Union some years ago. I had the feeling to call and see if the rebate was still valid; to my surprise, it was, and it reduced my new insurance in half. I was amazed and grateful for the different ways my needs were being met. I could comfortably afford both the car and the insurance for me, as well as for my two older ones.

Then I had to confront the lie of the gas shortage. Again, the creeping false suggestions of lack started, but my confidence in the ever-present provision of Love was there to help lift my thoughts to higher ground. I believed there could not be any shortages. I refused to limit the Allness of God on any front. I felt that since I was not using the car in any wasteful or extravagant way, I would have all that I needed. I drove out in a certain direction; the very first gas station had gas and only a few people at the pumps. I was grateful for this demonstration as well—evidence that God answers such reliance on Him.

I have been thinking: if I want to live the freedom that is my birthright, I must be willing to be an expression of God's nature. If I say I want to end a bad habit and still have the desire to indulge in it, it is dishonesty—and God is not present in that. Dishonesty has never been found where honesty is. Each day starts with my choice of which way I want my thinking to go. If I choose to stick with the spiritual Truth, I know my steps will be ordered.

It is time to challenge some of the accepted misconceptions in the name of culture or the notion of *just the way things are*. When a taxi driver is rude, people often say, "Well, that is New York City. That is how things are," implying that we must accept it. These are falsehoods. New York is also part of God's universe. If He is everywhere, then He is in New York as well. The people there are all His, whether they acknowledge it or not. In such instances, it is important to refute these false claims and replace them with the Truth.

Allowing such seemingly harmless assertions to go unchecked permits more significant misconceptions to influence our perception of New York. If we let every erroneous thought pass, we risk losing sight of the reality of universal harmony. Casual acceptance of untruth is merely an excuse, and we need not dwell in that space or suffer its woes.

To experience lasting peace and freedom, it is clear we must heed the moral dimension of Life. The root of our troubles lies in ignorance of moral obligation and the wilful disobedience of it. No amount of regulation, however well enforced, can serve as powerfully as an awakened conscience, one that can no longer tolerate wrongthinking and wrongdoing.

When executives embezzle, they know the consequences, but they do it anyway. When husbands are unfaithful, they are aware of the possible fallout, but they do it anyway. When people on parole break the law, it is not because they do not know what could happen.

This only confirms the limited power of material systems to guide us toward right action.

What, then, makes us do wrong even when we know better? What can truly stop us? It has been proven that the only lasting deterrent is a state of consciousness that refuses to entertain wrongdoing. Any human punishment will always be limited in its power to prevent wrong. It is moral transformation, not fear of penalty, which leads us to do right.

Yet the power of right consciousness makes any wrong action glaringly uncomfortable to carry out. I have heard people speak of moments when they were about to do something wrong, and they say "something" told them not to go through with it. That "something" is Christ's direct communication with one's consciousness. The more we cherish this communion and strive to keep our thoughts clear enough to listen and willing enough to follow, the more able we are to discern the right choice.

Thieves know the consequences of stealing. Cheaters know the consequences of cheating. Teenagers are aware of the possible outcomes of sexual activity. And yet, many still indulge in these acts, rendering punishment an ineffective deterrent. But the laws of God are higher, and we continue to suffer from disobedience to them, and at times from ignorance of them. How can we truly help in such situations?

What I used to think was sin was only a small part of what sin really is. Every time I accept the reality of any discord, I sin, and I suffer for it, whether through anxiety, fear, or confusion. In that moment, I had sided with wrong thinking, with the belief that there is something other than the infinite God. The solution to this suffering begins when we grow weary of self-condemnation and choose instead to repent—not only of the act, but of the false belief that gave rise to it. In humility, we must decide to forsake the lie and replace it with Love.

If I suspect someone is doing wrong, that thought only conjures up fear, doubt, and anxiety. But if I quickly settle the matter by affirming that there is only God, my thinking reflects the purity of God—and that brings peace and rest. It is vitally important to address any wrong that presents itself to thought. If I feel uneasy about something, I ought to pray to know what needs to be known about the situation. Spiritually discerning a wrong and rebuking it, in whichever way I am led, can save someone. God will care for all His children; only His Truth can purify.

During the 2008 election, I was working to keep my thoughts centred on Love. I did quite well throughout the day, but when I watched the news, I would start to criticize the candidates. I felt I was justified and made excuses to continue the habit. But I began to feel uneasy, and I did not like the anxious feeling. I searched deeply to uncover what unreality I had accepted as real.

Then one night, I realised that each time I criticised, I was indulging in wrong thinking rather than loving. It was right not to accept the wrong qualities being expressed, but my responsibility was to see the Truth about God's man, not to criticise and condemn. This is not easy, as the common tendency is to condemn the person instead of separating the behaviour and rebuking *it*.

I should always lift my thoughts to God for the light to shine on what I need to know about Him, something that will vanquish the darkness. As we all know, at the entry of light, darkness has no chance. Therefore, it is worth having my light ready to shine, so that the darkness never has a chance to frighten or disturb me.

Have you ever been to a party where everyone thinks they are being nice to you by asking you what you do, so that they can judge you before they get to know you? This happened to me when I visited the United States with a friend once. His parents were academicians, and they had a party at Christmas. Well, all these people wanted to know what this African girl did for work. Some of them would not even ask my name before asking what I did.

In order not to be too obvious, some of them cleverly asked if I attended university. In this indirect way of inquiring about my profession or occupation, they sought to categorise me, before even learning my name. Some of them missed the opportunity to know a genuinely nice person, simply because they were so concerned about status.

Such things should be secondary to the more important matters of life. If God is no respecter of persons, then we should not be so prejudiced and discriminating. " . . . . of a truth I perceive that God is no respecter of persons: But in every nation he that feareth him, and worketh righteousness, is accepted with him" (Acts 10: 34-35).

We judge others before they even speak, and this happens everywhere. Even in my country, we discriminate by tribe, and some judge by colour.

It makes me seem unintelligent to continue judging others based on tribal affiliation. I think of what God asked Job: whether he had been there when God created man. The answer, of course, is no. That alone should remind us that none of us has the audacity to judge anyone on such a superficial basis.

I must point out that such prejudice is not limited to the United States. When I was growing up in Ghana, I was aware of the lower esteem given to people from different tribes. Those who came from the northern part of Ghana were often viewed as unenlightened and were excluded from certain activities. There was a sense of superiority based on tribe.

It is true that, at times, these prejudices stem from differences in attitudes and beliefs. But if those beliefs are wrong, we must recognise that they are not a part of the real person. The unfortunate reality is that many people believed, and still believe, that such prejudices are true.

Globally, there is a wicked perpetuation of the idea that some people are superior, while others are expected to accept the lie of inferiority. People may be fooled into believing they are superior because of their tribe or skin colour, but we do not have to be in the dream with them, believing we are inferior because of it.

If we were to return to the spiritual facts about God's sons and daughters, and understand the Truth about our real selfhood, we would always regain our sense of true inheritance and rise above the lies.

Another area in which I have realised peace is the challenge of making decisions. I used to be scared I would make the wrong choice. That fear stemmed from not truly understanding who I was. You may have the same uncertainty.

Here is a letter I once sent to a friend who was about to make a big decision; it may give you some insight into my approach to decision-making.

"It comes to me to share with you what has helped with decisions. I don't make any! I just know. I have had to take certain actions, but they were easier to follow when I just knew."

One day, when I was trying to make a decision, I heard the following clearly: "When God is talking, there is no confusion." This calmed my thoughts, and soon things unfolded perfectly.

Try to keep personal opinions, experiences, human will, fears , and doubts out of the equation. Know that God communicates with everyone, regardless of race, colour, or educational background. God is infinite, and all His children, everywhere, can understand Him.

If Love is speaking to all of us all the time, then we should ensure that Love is all we are hearing. This is true for everyone, since we all have those moments when we sense, "something told me to do this or that." That *something* must be the still, small voice of Truth. When arguments or confusion arise, pray to know the absolute Truth of God's presence. You will be inspired as to what to do and shown the perfect way to do it. The outcome will be filled with blessings.

Many experiences show us that our thoughts either assure us of peace or rob us of harmony. At one gathering, where lovely food was being served and everyone seemed to be enjoying themselves, a preacher's wife sat looking rather unhappy. She refused all the dishes offered, and when asked why, she replied that everything being served would upset her stomach.

I could hardly believe that someone could, by her own thoughts, imprison herself to that extent. She did not eat a single thing that was served. In addition, her face held a strained, unhappy look. I wonder what would have happened if she had not believed that everything would upset her. I am sure that, had she eaten anything, her thinking would have immediately proven her belief correct—that every dish was unsuitable.

In the Gospel of Mathew 7:21, we read, "Not everyone that saith unto me Lord, Lord, shall enter into the kingdom of heaven; but he that doeth the will of my Father which is in heaven." We all know people who profess the Word of God yet seem to experience continual trouble. Is it worth asking ourselves: are we truly being obedient to God?

When I understood that I could not be obedient to two opposite views at the same time, I finally grasped what it meant to serve only one master. In John 12:26, we read, "If any man serve me, let him follow me; and where I am, there shall also my servant be; if any man serve me, him will my Father honour." If we dwell with God, where can our troubles be? We cannot entertain thoughts filled with the lies of sickness and woe, and at the same time, claim we honour God.

Jesus said, "I am the way, the truth, and the life: no man cometh to the Father, but by me" (John 14:6). He showed us He is the way. In James 4:7-8, we read, "Submit yourselves therefore to God, Resist the devil and he will flee from you. Draw nigh to God, and he will draw nigh to you. Cleanse your hands, ye sinners; and purify your hearts, ye double-minded." This double-mindedness arises when we affirm that God is All, yet simultaneously accept that the headache we feel is real, or that a wound on the leg must be lived with, or that a diagnosis of diabetes defines us. There is no middle ground. I must stay on the side of good, even when doing so may seem to cost some comfort for a while.

In Romans 6:16, we read, "Know ye not, that to whom ye yield yourselves servants to obey, his servants ye are to whom ye obey; whether of sin unto death, or of obedience unto righteousness?" Servants are dominated by their masters. So I am not surprised that, if I allow myself to believe in the falsity of discord, I become its servant.

In Deuteronomy 4:30-31, we read, " . . . if thou turn to the Lord thy God, and shalt be obedient unto His voice; . . . .he will not forsake thee." This is a powerful assurance—both of what we are to do, and of the promise that follows our obedience.

Sometimes, I felt almost paralysed by wrong thoughts that dominated my thinking. When I was meant to do something but felt discouraged, the entire project would be at risk—simply because I had allowed myself to believe the lie that I could not go on.

I had to change my thinking and replace those devastating thoughts with the Truth: that no matter what is happening, I am never separated from God. I must be mindful of what I am taking in at any moment and choose to dwell in the house of the Lord in order to receive the many blessings found there.

None of us needs to be afraid. We do not have to subject ourselves to illnesses, injustice, or mistreatment of any kind, because, as Job 22:29 says, "When men are cast down, then thou shalt say, There is lifting up; and he shall save the humble person." We do not have to fear if we know that God is All.

Do I hold on to wrong thoughts about someone who has offended me? Do I readily challenge the false suggestions of bodily pains? Do I sometimes like to cling to these claims in order to gain sympathy or attention? What price do I pay for this tenacious obedience to the so-called laws of sin and death? How much am I truly willing to give up in order to find my Life in Christ?

When the belief of illness appears, we do all we can to rid ourselves of the discomfort—yet we may still hold on to the very sinful beliefs that invite such suffering. At times, we even refuse to release those beliefs, excusing ourselves by saying that they have been a part of us for years, even though they clearly trespass on the laws of God.

In Isaiah 54:17, we read, "No weapon that is formed against thee shall prosper; and every tongue that shall rise against thee in judgment thou shalt condemn. This is the heritage of the servants of the Lord, and their righteousness is of me, saith the Lord." Such is the great prize for those who earnestly strive to understand God.

In the Book of Romans, 8:35, 37 says, "Who shall separate us from the love of Christ? Shall tribulation, or distress, or persecution, or famine, or nakedness, or peril, or sword? Nay, in all these things we are more than conquerors through him that loved us." This assures me that, even when I feel afraid or discouraged, my higher sense must remind me that I am never separated from God.

We keep searching, because only the higher things of Spirit can truly satisfy. Did we really think we could solve our problems in any other way? We are urged to hold fast to this understanding that preserves our liberty. In Galatians 5:1, "Stand fast therefore in the liberty wherewith Christ hath made us free, and be not entangled again with the yoke of bondage." And again, the promise is clear: "And ye shall know the truth and the truth shall make you free" (John 8:32).

Another way we can hold to the Truth is by sharing, with Love, what we have come to realise. In Galatians 5:13, we read, "For, brethren, ye have been called unto liberty for an occasion to flesh, but by love serve one another."

The only way to overcome evil of any kind is to turn completely from its seeming reality and to replace it with a conviction of our purity as children of God. This is the obedience that truly sets us free.

Changing locations or jobs is useful only to the extent that it helps us replace the false belief in evil with the Truth of God's allness. Without that inner shift, external change cannot offer lasting peace.

I once tried—through sheer willpower—to manage money more wisely, but I could not. I changed banks many times. Each time, it began well, but sooner or later, fear crept in, or the inability to maintain correct balances returned. Old mistakes would resurface in thought and, before long—*voila!*—The whole situation would spiral again.

It was not until I prayed, surrendering my will to fix things, and wholeheartedly accepted my complete perfection as including every good, that I finally witnessed lasting change. The belief had been that *I am a person who cannot manage money*. But this was false. God has had everything complete from the beginning. Now, someone might say it is ridiculous that an educated woman with a law degree could not manage her finances.

To any such comment, I would ask: Have you ever searched yourself? Is there one thing that has so mesmerised you that you completely believe it? Have you tried everything—positive thinking included—to get rid of it, only to find that traces still remain? It could be drinking, smoking, lusting after women, gambling, choosing the wrong partners, fear, false appetites—this is the kind of false identification I am referring to.

To recognise the wrong is good. Then, let the Truth of correct self-identification do the work. Humbly acknowledge—with a grateful, loving heart—the Truth about yourself. Insist on this Truth until it vanquishes every trace of the lie that would deny God's own reflection. My false picture was telling me I was not the expression of God. What a lie when Perfection knows not the slightest imperfection. We have been promised the peace of God, which passes all understanding, if we are doing right. We must protect this peace and let nothing take it from us. Peace is the only precious possession we have.

The more I understand Jesus's mission through the writings of Mrs. Eddy, the more clearly and deeply I appreciate what he suffered for all mankind. He left us with the knowledge of what a precious gift we have as children of God—and how vitally important it is for us to love and safeguard that reality.

We love God best when we are obedient to what He knows about each of His children. Nothing else can help us as much as an individual and collective effort to know ourselves and each other as spiritual beings. Any other form of identification falls short of the purity that includes all that is good.

If we say we are mortals, then we accept the belief that some are more intelligent than others. But we have all been given the ability to fulfil our purpose here and now. If we identify first with a particular race, with our human families, or a certain geographical region, we also identify with whatever limitations or negatives may seem to come with them. Our spiritual identity is our only true identity. We must be grateful for it and love it enough to see both ourselves and others in that light.

To love God enough to place complete confidence in His protecting care accomplishes more than even our most determined efforts to fix things humanly.

Redemption and reformation alone bring peace. It is interesting that, despite all we know from Scripture urging us to seek God first, many still feel they might miss out on something by obeying this commandment. As a result, many people only come to embrace it later in life.

Galatians 5:1, 13 says, "Stand fast therefore in the liberty wherewith Christ hath made us free, and be not entangled again with the yoke of bondage . . . For, brethren, ye have been called unto liberty;" This does not mean we can *make* the Truth set us free through effort alone. Instead, we must be willing to remain within God's laws—for it is through them that our freedom is revealed.

Our promise of freedom is contingent on a practical knowledge of God. This must involve consistently familiarizing ourselves with His commandments and firmly establishing in thought God's omnipotence, omnipresence, omniscience, and omni-action.

Each morning, I make a point to affirm the power and magnificence of His love, that He alone is governing all. Psalm 121 contains verses that help me recognise His presence and involvement in everything the day holds. So when I step outside, I do so with the quiet confidence that God is with everyone else, too. Wherever I go—every store, every car, at every meeting—Christ is already there. This way of thinking brings harmony, and I am grateful for it. Such is the peace available to all mankind.

There was a time when it seemed our whole household was engaged in the search for the correct position. My husband needed a change from his previous profession, as it no longer fulfilled him. It had become clear that his true passion—and the area in which he was most gifted—had not been fully utilised. So, in many ways, this crossroads was not a bad thing.

My daughter, talented in various aspects of film production, was also searching for her niche within the industry. I, meanwhile, was working in a role that aligned with my highest sense of service, but the remuneration felt inadequate, especially now that my husband was not working.

I prayed with the Truths I knew and with the spiritual insights shared by a Christian Science Practitioner (someone devoted full-time to the healing practice of prayer from a spiritual perspective). Yet many mornings were filled with sadness, impatience, and even flashes of anger. I struggled with a false sense of responsibility—one I did not want. I felt I had done the best to know the Truth, and it seemed unjust to feel accountable for someone else's understanding of it.

There was no usual talking around the house, especially with my husband. I realised there was no joy in our home, and I knew that was wrong. I had allowed myself to be brought low by something that was clearly untrue. From my study of the Bible and *Science and Health*, I knew not to believe what I was seeing.

One morning, with tears in my eyes, these questions came to me: "When my patients are sad, do I become sad with them? When they are impatient or depressed, do I grow impatient and depressed, too?" The answer is *no*. I take the position of God's ever-presence and refuse to accept the presented picture that someone is depressed. In those moments, I turn to any hymn, psalm, or Bible verse, or to a passage from *Science and Health,* which will lift my thought and restore the joy that is always mine in Truth.

So, I took my books and went for a walk to the park, where I had previously found much peace simply pondering the Truth. There, I reflected on how foolish it is to continue in disobedience to God and thereby prolong our suffering—especially when, time and again, the Bible warns us not to trust the material sense of things.

The realisation of the Truth about what I had allowed to preoccupy my thoughts brought healing to our household. My husband found a more suitable position, and so did my daughter. I began receiving more calls for my services, and our supply was adequately met.

One last reminder about prayer: it is that quiet communion with God which helps us feel better, think clearly, and do better. It provides the right thinking that enables us to correct the false impressions we may hold about ourselves, others, or Life situations. It is not the loud declaration of words, meant only to impress, that avails much. Rather, it is the sincere desire and earnest longing to hear God, to love Him, and to obey His will.

Persistent engagement in this practice enables us to reflect the Mind of Christ. It brings thoughts of comfort, strength, courage, reassurance, trust, and conviction in God's ever-present power. We can do this anywhere—in the kitchen, the shower, at work, on the bus, and even amid a crowd.

Let us not forget, or underestimate, the impact of this correct thinking; it has a profound effect on the overall world thought. It awakens us to what wrong thoughts need to be cast out. It helps us to see the good God sees and thus positively influence our experiences. Thus, the admonition to pray without ceasing.

In Galatians 3:3, we are warned of this. "Are ye so foolish? Having begun in the Spirit, are ye now made perfect by the flesh?"

As Paul says, "... .for the things which are seen are temporal; but the things which are not seen are eternal" (2 Corinthians 4:18). We should look to the eternal freedom that is not dependent on anything material. If this is our heart's desire, then it's time to see ourselves as God sees us.

"Human life is like that film; there is a story going on that screen, and though the producer may be hammering some theme at you, it is up to you to accept it or reject it. You just sit there, with your standard of judgment and good sense within you, and accordingly, you are influenced by that film or not.

"We should know that man is not what he looks like, or what he feels like, but that he is in essence just qualities, good qualities, and we should look for those and bring them out" (*The Science of Man*, Morgan, p. 8).

"Citizens of the world, accept the glorious liberty of the children of God, and be free! This is your divine right." (*Science and Health*, Eddy, pg. 227:24-26).

True freedom awaits us all. I do not know a better way to understand God and ourselves—and to begin experiencing this true and eternal freedom.

Hymn 412
The Christian Science Hymnal, 1932 edition
by Rosa Turner

O dreamer, leave thy dreams for joyful waking,
O captive, rise and sing for thou art free;
The Christ is here, all dreams of error breaking,
Unloosing bonds of all captivity.

He comes to bless thee on His wings of healing;
To banish pain, and wipe all tears away;
He comes anew, to humble hearts, revealing
The mounting footsteps of the upward way.

He comes to give thee joy for desolation,
Beauty for ashes of the vanished years;
For every tear to bring full compensation,
To give thee confidence for all thy fears.

He comes to call the dumb to joyful singing;
The deaf to hear; the blinded eyes to see;
The glorious tidings of salvation are bringing.
O captive, rise, thy Saviour comes to thee.

ACKNOWLEDGEMENTS

I am grateful that my parents made the teachings of the Bible so significant in our lives. That background formed the basis for what I am learning through Christian Science. Thanks to my husband, Kofi, and our three children for being patient with me when I did not know where I was going with this new way of thinking, and they did not understand my actions. I thank my sister, Efua, for being the first to urge me to explore Christian Science with her, after our father's healing. I also thank all the practitioners whose help I have sought along the way. My most sincere thanks to the independent practitioner/teacher whose love and strength gave me what I was yearning for to go forward to study and live this Science in the right way. Her teaching helped me to examine my thoughts often, to keep my thoughts focused on God, and to have God in all the details of my life.

My sincere thanks to Karen Marshall for proofreading and some editing of this edition.

Last, I thank every sincere seeker of Truth who may be led to this book. If just one insight from it leads you to start your own study of your Bible with *Science and Health with Key to the Scriptures* by Mary Baker Eddy, God only knows how many lives your living the Truth can touch and change. Together, the whole brotherhood of man can realise our true selves and our true freedom.

Appendix: Visit www.plainfieldcs.com for more information about Mary Baker Eddy and Christian Science. For any comments or questions, please email: Greatergood365@gmail.com.

Thanks again to all my readers.

BIBLIOGRAPHY

The Holy Bible, King James Version

Eddy, Mary Baker. *Science and Health with Key to the Scriptures.*1910 Boston: The Christian Science Publishing Society.

Rieke, Herbert E. "Discovering Peaceful Relationships." Presentation at the New York World's Fair on July 26, 1964.

Tomlinson, Irving. *Twelve Years with Mary Baker Eddy: Recollections and Experiences*. Boston: The Christian Science Publishing Society, 1945. Additional articles by Irving Tomlinson.

Wilcox, Martha. *The True Relationship of God and Man*. Santa Clarita, CA: The Bookmark, 2002. Articles by Martha Wilcox.

Morgan, John L. *The Science of Man*. London: Foundational Book Co., 1957

Eddy, Mary Baker. *Miscellaneous Writings*, in *Prose Works*. Boston: First Church Of Christ, Scientist, 1953.

Kratzer, Glen. *Dominion Within*. Santa Clarita: The Bookmark, 2003. Articles by Rev. G.A. Kratzer.

Drummond, Henry, and Harold J. Chadwick. *The Greatest Thing in The World: Love*. New Jersey: Bridge-Logos, 1999.

For additional helpful books and articles, visit: https://members.plainfieldcs.com/publications-page/

Additional Resources

For those interested in exploring these practical insights further, the Plainfield Christian Science Church, Independent, offers many of these foundational texts and additional spiritual resources to support your study and practice.

ABOUT THE AUTHOR

Florence was raised in a Christian family in a small seaside town in Ghana, West Africa. She later moved to England, where she received her medical nursing, midwifery, and public health nursing certificates. Once in the United States, she earned a degree in nursing and a law degree.

After her father's stroke and subsequent remarkable recovery through Christian Science healing, Florence embarked on the study of this preventative and curative Truth. She joined the healing ministry of Christian Science and worked as a Christian Science nurse for nine years. She is currently a Christian Science practitioner; someone who aids anyone caught up in a problem to apply God's Truth to bring about resolution and healing.

She shares her experiences and what she continues to learn with other Truth seekers, to help inspire and encourage others to explore the healing Truth and practice of Christian Science. Applying spiritual insights from that study to her everyday life has given her a new view of herself, others, and an overall transforming perspective on life.

It is her sincerest desire that what she shares will impel others to conduct their own study of these two life-changing books: The Bible and *Science and Health with Key to the Scriptures* by Mary Baker Eddy. She works each day to practice what she is learning about man's true freedom. She lives in Atlanta, Georgia, with her husband. They have three children.